CW00486124

A Series of Lessons
in Raja Yoga

Yogi Ramacharaka

A Series of Lessons
in Raja Yoga

Yogi Ramacharaka

Bamboo Leaf Press

Copyright © 2022, by Bamboo Leaf Press
Copyright © 1906, 1907, 1934, by The Yogi Publication Society

All rights reserved. This book or any portion thereof may not be re-
produced or used in any manner whatsoever without the express
written permission of the publisher except for the use of brief quotations in a book review.

ISBN 978-0-9974148-7-5
eBook ISBN 978-0-9974148-8-2

Published by Bamboo Leaf Press,
London, UK and New York, USA
www.bambooleafpress.com

The Yogi Ramacharaka book series was originally published between 1903 and 1909 by the Yogi Publication Society in Chicago. These books, particularly *Fourteen Lessons in Yogi Philosophy and Oriental Occultism, Advanced Course in Yogi Philosophy and Oriental Occultism,* and *A Series of Lessons in Raja Yoga,* had a profound influence on my outlook on life. Although I had been exposed to Eastern ideas in my early twenties through practicing Hatha yoga, the Yogi Ramacharaka books served as a foundation that prompted a deeper investigation into yogi philosophy, one that has opened a new perspective to the world.

Almost 120 years have passed since the initial publication of the Yogi Ramacharaka books. Yet still, in my opinion, these books remain the best introduction to Eastern philosophy and spirituality. Presented as lessons to Westerners curious about the East, the written language is straightforward, and the abstract ideas are easy to understand. The lesson format also makes the material approachable, with each lesson building upon the previous. And the overall style of a teacher directly addressing a student is in harmony with the traditions of the East, where a guru teaches a pupil (or "sadhaka"). In fact, these books were originally designed as lessons for a correspondence course in monthly installments, later gathered and published as individual books.

There are a few elements of style that point to another mindset and time period, which may disturb some readers. For example, only masculine pronouns are used in the texts, and some cultural references are extremely dated, revealing a divergence from what we today consider to be politically correct. I have addressed these instances in the Endnotes. I decided, however, to preserve the integrity of the original writing style as well as the author's voice because I think that a significant part of the charm of these books is their *fin de siècle* flavor. Therefore, apart from updating spelling errors and including a few missing words, only minimal edits were made.

There are several instances where Yogi Ramacharaka refers to his own contemporaries, some of whom are well known, like H.G. Wells, and others more obscure, such as "Prof. Masson." What information I have found on these figures, I have included in the Endnotes.

I am especially grateful to the yoga teacher and writer Richard Rosen, who graciously agreed to include an adapted version of his detective work on Yogi Ramacharaka's identity. A big thank you to the most creative book designer Poppy Alexiou for breathing new life into these wonderful books. To writer Nicos Hadjicostis, my partner, I owe a deep gratitude for his persistent encouragement and endless support in bringing this project to fruition.

Jane Kayantas
Bamboo Leaf Press
January 2022

Foreword

Who was Yogi Ramacharaka?

And in the home of the novelist
There is a satin-like bow on an harp.
You enter and pass hall after hall,
Conservatory follows conservatory,
Lilies lift their white symbolical cups,
Whence their symbolical pollen has been excerpted,
Near them I noticed an harp
And the blue satin ribbon,
And the copy of Hatha Yoga.
    – Ezra Pound, from *Moeurs Contemporaines V* (1919)

Hatha Yoga is an actual book, not a product of the poet's imagination. I can say this with confidence because I have a copy, bought at a used book store for $15. Subtitled *The Yogi Philosophy of Physical Well-Being*, it was first published, remarkably enough, in 1904, one of the first—if not *the* first—books written about Hatha Yoga in English for a popular audience. The title page attributes the work to a Yogi Ramacharaka who, from 1903 to 1909, churned out fourteen books on subjects ranging from Hindu philosophy and yoga to Oriental occultism, mystic Christianity, life after death and reincarnation, and the "science of psychic healing."

Who was Yogi Ramacharaka? His first publisher, the Yogi Publication Society, which in the early 1900s was headquartered in

Chicago, tells the following story about him: Born in India around 1799, Yogi Ramacharaka, like several of the seekers in this book, ventured out early in life to hunt for the Truth. He spent many years trudging back and forth across "the East," fasting, meditating, and digging through the libraries of countless lamaseries and monasteries. Around 1865, after having passed what must have been a good forty years on his quest, Yogi Ramacharaka finally discovered the unnamed "basis for his philosophy." At about the same time, he acquired a student, the eight-year-old son of a Brahmin family, whom we know as Baba Bharata. Yogi Ramacharaka then resumed his peripatetic ways, retracing the steps of his life's journey, this time with little Baba in tow.

We next hear about the wanderers almost thirty years later, in 1893. Now 94, and sensing that he would soon shuffle off his mortal coil, Yogi Ramacharaka deputized Baba to spread his teaching near and far. You may recall that in that year, the World's Parliament of Religions convened in Chicago as part of the World's Fair. Baba realized that such a gathering would make the perfect bully pulpit, so off he went to the US. His appearance at the Parliament was, according to the Yoga Publication Society, an "instant success." He lectured before enthusiastic audiences from all parts of the world who were visiting the Fair, attracting a considerable following in the process. Many wished him to start a new religion—but he felt only the urge to write about Yogi Ramacharaka and his teaching.

While he might have been an effective, even charismatic speaker, Baba wasn't much of a writer. Fortunately he met one William Walker Atkinson, described as an "English author," and despite their divergent backgrounds, they apparently recognized in each other a fellow traveler. They agreed to pool their talents and write books, Baba contributing his guru's hard-earned wisdom, Atkinson his talent with words. It seemed only proper that they signed their joint efforts "Yogi Ramacharaka."

It's a touching tale but with a big hole that's hard to plug: there's absolutely no record that a Baba Bharata addressed the Parliament, though as we know Baba Premananda Bharati with-a-final-"i" arrived in New York City around 1902. Some people have jumped to the conclusion that, just because the story doesn't exactly add up, Baba was only a figment of someone's vivid imagination. This is certainly a possibility and we will be explaining it further down. So if these two gentlemen were fictitious, who wrote those fourteen books?

The only name left standing from the Yogi Publication Society story is the ghost writer, "English author" William Walker Atkinson, who was both a real person and an author. But why the Yogi Publication Society called him English is a mystery—maybe what they meant is that he *wrote* in English, because Atkinson was born and raised in Baltimore. Around 1890 he had become a successful businessman and lawyer, but success, as it still often does today, took a toll. In his late 20s or early 30s (it's not clear exactly when), he experienced some kind of debilitating breakdown (what exactly happened isn't spelled out, but it seems he suffered what we would call "professional burnout") and financial ruination.

In those far-off days before the ready availability of sympathetic though pricey therapists and mood-altering drugs, Atkinson decided to take the proverbial bull by the horns. He pulled himself out of his funk with the help of techniques he learned from a popular self-help movement known variously as New Thought, Mental Science, Mind Cure, the Boston Craze, and Practical Christianity. Eager to join and help promote the vehicle of his miraculously restored physical, psychic, and financial health, Atkinson moved to the ground zero of New Thought activity, Chicago, sometime in the late 1890s.

It didn't take long for him to hop aboard the bandwagon. By 1900, he was an associate editor of the New Thought magazine *Suggestion* and had published his first book, *Thought-Force in Business and Everyday Life*. Through his involvement with New Thought, which was heavily influenced by what today is called Neo-Vedanta, it seemed that Atkinson had also delved deep into Indian philosophy. He could draw on several scholarly and popular books for background material, though much of what was found in the latter was misinformed about India and Indians, yet this was enough to build a good foundation of knowledge about Eastern philosophy. He seems, though, to have stuck with relatively reliable sources, since here and there in Yogi Ramacharaka's books we come across quotes from nineteenth-century Indologists like the well-known German scholar Max Müller (who also addressed the World Parliament of Religions on "Greek Philosophy and the Christian Religion"), fellow German Paul Deussen, American Sanskrit scholar Edward Washburn Hopkins, and Englishman Monier Monier-Williams.

Technically, Atkinson was responsible for nearly forty books (he also cowrote another twenty), which nowadays would be shelved in the Self-Help, New Age/Occult, or even the Business sections of the bigger national chain stores. His interests were eclectic, to say the least, and most of us would agree somewhat out of the ordinary, unless your usual reading fare includes books about personal magnetism and the "magnetic gaze," telepathy, practical mental influence and mind reading, practical psychic training—an umbrella term that covers psychometry (the technique of divining information about people or events related to an object solely by touching or being close to it), intuition, clairvoyance, psychomancy (divination with the help of spirits), and crystal gazing—the "science of observing, remembering, and recalling," self-healing by "thought force," the art of logical thinking, the psychology of salesmanship, reincarnation and the "law of karma," and more. Believe it or not, Atkinson's 1906 book, *Thought Vibra-*

tion or The Law of Attraction in the Thought World, was a major inspiration for the 2006 popular book and movie *The Secret* (according to its author/producer Rhonda Byrne) that has since become a big movement. Atkinson was a truly remarkable person. His preoccupation with so many diverse fields of knowledge and the seriousness with which he delved into his studies and spiritual seekings have resulted in an oeuvre that is still relevant to our modern world.

By now you've probably guessed that Atkinson himself is the best candidate for being the mysterious Yogi Ramacharaka. But not so fast! We first have to reply to the question: Why go through all the trouble to pretend to be writing for a nonexistent person? One possible reason is that Atkinson felt books about Indian philosophy and yoga would gain credence with his readers if they thought they were written by a yogi. But some Yogi Ramacharaka aficionados believe Atkinson was truly tutored in the finer points of Indian philosophy by Baba Bharati, or that he traveled to India and studied with a yogi—the latter being very unlikely. Others have claimed that Atkinson's "Baba" was Swami Vivekananda. However, while the two might have been in the same general vicinity in Chicago or Baltimore, there's no concrete evidence that they ever met or corresponded. One other possible teacher whom I've never seen mentioned before is an Indian scholar by the name of Manilal Dvivedi, who, like Vivekananda, was a delegate to the 1893 World Parliament. In the preface to *The Spirit of the Upanishads* (1907), Yogi Ramacharaka "acknowledges his appreciation of the work of Dr. Manil N. Dvivedi ... the original translator" of many of the approximately 420 aphorisms. I wasn't able to find out anything more about this relationship, if that's the right word, and we probably will never know if Atkinson had a live tutor, although he may have.

And still, the mystery remains because the Yogi Ramacharaka

books are markedly different from Atkinson's other books. When Jane Kayantas of Bamboo Leaf Press asked me to provide the present biography, she mentioned her ideas about Atkinson collaborating with another person to write the books and presented strong points to support her case. First, Jane focused on the writing style. She contends that the Yogi Ramacharaka books are written in a completely different voice than Atkinson's other books. But the books aren't just different, they are *significantly better*, with a more condensed, clear, and methodical writing style than that found in Atkinson's other books. Second, the voice of the Ramacharaka books reveals a deep understanding of Eastern philosophy, particularly of the Vedanta. This is especially evident in another Yogi Ramacharaka book, *Philosophies and Religions of India*, which Bamboo Leaf Press may publish in the future. In the *Philosophies* book, the writer's (or writers') thorough knowledge and understanding of the various religions of India is impressive. The writer's high level of expertise goes well beyond the standard Theosophical and New Age writings of the period and certainly surpasses the content found in Atkinson's other, much weaker books. Which brings us to the third and probably the most important point: How is it that *all* of the Yogi Ramacharaka books have remained relevant and in print after 120 years, but most other books authored only by Atkinson and his other pseudonyms have nearly vanished (with the exception of *Thought Vibration*)? It seems that these books have some special quality, and this quality may truly be none other than that which Atkinson himself claimed to have been: the contribution of another writer more knowledgeable than him in Eastern philosophy, a person who may have given the books their very unique language and style not to be found in Atkinson's other books. So, while "Baba Bharata" may have never been identified, the reference may actually be to a well-versed yogi who helped Atkinson cowrite the Yogi Ramacharaka series. I have to admit that Jane has a quite strong case. We may, therefore, conclude that although Atkinson was almost certainly the main author, many of the philosophical ideas contained in these books may have been provided in big part by a mystery collaborator who was well versed in Eastern Philosophy.

Richard Rosen
Yoga Teacher and Writer

The seven main chakra symbols on the left are the featured design elements throughout the book. Chakra in Sanskrit means "wheel" or "disk". These symbols are prevalent in Hindu and Buddhist iconography. Chakras are the body's energy centers that begin at the base of the spine and move upwards to the crown of the head. Each chakra is associated with a specific psychological, spiritual, and physical aspect of our life. Unbalanced or blocked chakras may result in illnesses and disorders. Balanced chakras lead to well-being and good health, which may be achieved with yoga practice.

Contents

The Original Publisher's Note

The lessons which compose this volume, originally appeared in the shape of monthly lessons, the first of which was issued in October, 1905, and the twelfth in September, 1906. These lessons met with a hearty and generous response from the public, and the present volume is issued in response to the demand for the lessons in a permanent and durable form. There have been no changes made in the text.

The publishers take the liberty to call the attention of the reader to the great amount of information condensed within the space given to each lesson. Students have told us that they have found it necessary to read and study each lesson carefully, in order to absorb the varied information contained within its pages. They have also stated that they have found it advisable to reread the lessons several times, allowing an interval between each reading and that at each rereading they would discover information that had escaped them during the course of the previous study. This has been repeated to us so often that we feel justified in mentioning it, that other readers might avail themselves of the same course and plan of study.

Following his usual custom, the writer of the lessons has declined to write a preface for this book, claiming that the lessons speak for themselves, and that those for whom they are intended will receive the message contained within them, without any prefatory talk.

Yogi Publication Society
Oak Park, Illinois
September 1, 1906

"When the soul sees itself as a Center
surrounded by its circumference
—when the Sun knows that it is a Sun,
surrounded by its whirling planets—
then is it ready for the Wisdom and Power
of the Masters."

The "I"

In India, the Candidates for Initiation into the science of Raja Yoga, when they apply to the Yogi Masters for instruction, are given a series of lessons designed to enlighten them regarding the nature of the Real Self, and to instruct them in the secret knowledge whereby they may develop the consciousness and realization of the real "I" within them. They are shown how they may cast aside the erroneous or imperfect knowledge regarding their real identity.

Until the Candidate masters this instruction, or at least until the truth becomes fixed in his consciousness, further instruction is denied him, for it is held that until he has awakened to a conscious realization of his Actual Identity, he is not able to understand the source of his power, and, moreover, is not able to *feel* within him the power of the Will, which power underlies the entire teachings of Raja Yoga.

The Yogi Masters are not satisfied if the Candidate forms merely a clear intellectual conception of this Actual Identity, but they insist that he must *feel* the truth of the same—must become *aware* of the Real Self—must enter into a consciousness in which the realization becomes a part of his everyday self—in which the realizing consciousness becomes the prevailing idea in his mind, around which his entire thoughts and actions revolve.

To some Candidates, this realization comes like a lightning flash the moment the attention is directed toward it, while in other cases the Candidates find it necessary to follow a rigorous course of training before they acquire the realization in consciousness.

The Yogi Masters teach that there are two degrees of this awakening consciousness of the Real Self. The first, which they call "the Consciousness of the 'I,'" is the full consciousness of *real* existence that comes to the Candidate, and which causes him to *know* that he is a real entity having a life not depending upon the body—life that will go on in spite of the destruction of the body—*real* life, in fact. The second degree, which they call "the Consciousness of the 'I AM,'" is the consciousness of one's identity with the Universal Life, and his relationship to, and "in-touchness" with all life, expressed and unexpressed. These two degrees of consciousness come in time to all who seek "The Path." To some it comes suddenly; to others it dawns gradually; to many it comes assisted by the exercises and practical work of Raja Yoga.

The first lesson of the Yogi Masters to the Candidates, leading up to the first degree, above mentioned, is as follows: That the Supreme Intelligence of the Universe—the Absolute—has manifested the being that we call Man—the highest manifestation on this planet. The Absolute has manifested an infinitude of forms of life in the Universe, including distant worlds, suns, planets, etc., many of these forms being unknown to us on this planet, and being impossible of conception by the mind of the ordinary man. But these lessons have nothing to do with that part of the philosophy which deals with these myriad forms of life, for our time will be taken up with the unfoldment in the mind of man of his true nature and power. Before man attempts to solve the secrets of the Universe without, he should master the Universe within—the Kingdom of the Self. When he has accomplished this, then he may, and should, go forth to gain the outer knowledge as a Master demanding its secrets, rather than as a slave begging for the crumbs from the table of knowledge. The first knowledge for the Candidate is the knowledge of the Self.

Man, the highest manifestation of the Absolute, as far as this planet is concerned, is a wonderfully organized being—although the average man understands but little of his real nature. He comprises within his physical, mental and spiritual makeup both the highest and the lowest, as we have shown in our previous lessons (the *Fourteen Lessons* and the *Advanced Course*). In his bones he manifests almost in the form of mineral life, in fact, in his bones, body and blood mineral substances actually exist. The physical life of the body resembles the life of the plant. Many of the physical desires and emotions are akin to those of the lower animals, and in the undeveloped man these desires and emotions predominate and overpower the higher nature, which latter is scarcely in evidence. Then Man has a set of mental characteristics that are his own, and which are not possessed by the lower animals (See *Fourteen Lessons*). And in addition to the mental faculties common to all men, or rather, that are in evidence in a greater or lesser degree among all men, there are still higher faculties latent within Man, which when manifested and expressed render Man more than ordinary Man.

The unfoldment of these latent faculties is possible to all who have reached the proper stage of development, and the desire and hunger of the student for this instruction is caused by the pressure of these unfolding latent faculties, crying to be born into consciousness. Then there is that wonderful thing, the Will, which is but faintly understood by those ignorant of the Yogi Philosophy—the Power of the Ego—its birthright from the Absolute.

But while these mental and physical things *belong* to Man, they are *not* the Man himself. Before the Man is able to master, control, and direct the things belonging to him—his tools and instruments—he must awaken to a realization of Himself. He must be able to distinguish between the "I" and the "Not I." And this is the first task before the Candidate.

That which is the Real Self of Man is the Divine Spark sent forth from the Sacred Flame. It is the Child of the Divine Parent. It is Immortal—Eternal—Indestructible—Invincible. It possesses within itself Power, Wisdom, and Reality. But like the infant that contains within itself the sometime Man, the mind of Man is unaware of its latent and potential qualities, and does not know itself. As it awakens and unfolds into the knowledge of its real nature, it manifests its qualities, and realizes what the Absolute has given it. When the Real Self begins to awaken, it sets aside from itself those things which are but appendages to it, but which it, in its half-waking state, had regarded as its Self. Setting aside first this, and then that, it finally discards all of the "Not I," leaving the Real Self free and delivered from its bondage to its appendages. Then it returns to the discarded appendages, and makes use of them.

In considering the question: "What is the Real Self?" let us first stop to examine what man usually means when he says "I."

The lower animals do not possess this "I" sense. They are conscious of the outer world; of their own desires and animal cravings and feelings. But their consciousness has not reached the Self-conscious stage. They are not able to think of themselves as separate entities, and to reflect upon their thoughts. They are not possessed of a consciousness of the Divine Spark—the Ego—the Real Self. The Divine Spark is hidden in the lower forms of life—even in the lower forms of human life—by many sheaths that shut out its light. But, nevertheless, it is there, always. It sleeps within the mind of the savage[1]—then, as he unfolds, it begins to throw out its light. In you, the Candidate, it is fighting hard to have its beams pierce through the material coverings. When the Real Self begins to arouse itself from its sleep, its dreams vanish from it, and it begins to see the world as it is, and to recognize itself in Reality and not as the distorted thing of its dreams.

The savage and barbarian are scarcely conscious of the "I." They are but a little above the animal in point of consciousness, and their "I" is almost entirely a matter of the consciousness of the wants of the body; the satisfaction of the appetites; the gratification of the passions; the securing of personal comfort; the expression of lust, savage power, etc. In the savage, the lower part of the Instinctive Mind is the seat of the "I." (See *Fourteen Lessons* for explanation of the several mental planes of man.) If the savage could analyze his thoughts, he would say that the "I" was the physical body, the said body having certain "feelings," "wants" and "desires." The "I" of such a man is a physical "I," the body representing its form and substance. Not only is this true of the savage, but even among so-called "civilized" men of today we find many in this stage. They have developed powers of thinking and reasoning, but they do not "live in their minds" as do some of their brothers. They use their thinking powers for the gratification of their bodily desires and cravings, and really live on the plane of the Instinctive Mind. Such a person may speak of "my mind," or "my soul," not from a high position where he looks upon these things from the standpoint of a Master who realizes his Real Self, but from below, from the point of view of the man who lives on the plane of the Instinctive Mind and who sees above *himself* the higher attributes. To such people the body is the "I." Their "I" is bound up with the senses, and that which comes to them through the senses. Of course, as Man advances in "culture" and "civilization," his senses become educated, and are satisfied only with more refined things, while the less cultivated man is perfectly satisfied with the more material and gross sense gratifications. Much that we call "cultivation" and "culture" is naught but a cultivation of a more refined form of sense gratification, instead of a real advance in consciousness and unfoldment. It is true that the advanced student and Master is possessed of highly developed senses, often far surpassing those of the ordinary man, but in such cases the senses have been cultivated under the mastery of the Will, and are made servants of the Ego instead of things hindering the progress of the soul—they are made servants instead of masters.

As Man advances in the scale, he begins to have a somewhat higher conception of the "I." He begins to use his mind and reason, and he passes on to the Mental Plane—his mind begins to manifest upon the plane of Intellect. He finds that there is something within him that is higher than the body. He finds that his mind seems more *real* to him than does the physical part of him, and in times of deep thought and study he is able almost to forget the existence of the body.

In this second stage, Man soon becomes perplexed. He finds problems that demand an answer, but as soon as he thinks he has answered them the problems present themselves in a new phase, and he is called upon to "explain his explanation." The mind, even although not controlled and directed by the Will, has a wonderful range, but, nevertheless, Man finds himself traveling around and around in a circle, and realizes that he is confronted continually by the Unknown. This disturbs him, and the higher the stage of "book learning" he attains, the more disturbed does he become. The man of but little knowledge does not see the existence of many problems that force themselves before the attention of the man of more knowledge, and demand an explanation from him. The tortures of the man who has attained the mental growth that enables him to see the new problems and the impossibility of their answer, cannot be imagined by one who has not advanced to that stage.

The man in this stage of consciousness thinks of his "I" as a mental thing, having a lower companion, the body. He feels that he has advanced, but yet his "I" does not give him the answer to the riddles and questions that perplex him. And he becomes most unhappy. Such men often develop into Pessimists, and consider the whole of life as utterly evil and disappointing—a curse rather than a blessing. Pessimism belongs to this plane, for neither the Physical Plane man or the Spiritual Plane man have this curse of Pessimism. The former man has no such disquieting thoughts, for he is almost entirely absorbed in gratifying his animal nature, while the latter man recognizes his mind as an instrument of himself, rather than as *himself*, and knows it to be imperfect in its present stage of growth. He knows that he has in himself the key to all knowledge—locked up in the Ego—and which the trained mind, cultivated, developed and guided by the awakened Will, may grasp as it unfolds. Knowing this the advanced man no longer despairs, and, recognizing his real nature, and his possibilities, as he awakens into a consciousness of his powers and capabilities, he laughs at the old despondent, pessimistic ideas, and discards them like a worn-out garment. Man on the Mental Plane of consciousness is like a huge elephant who knows not his own strength. He could break down barriers and assert himself over nearly any condition or environment, but in his ignorance of his real condition and power he may be mastered by a puny driver, or frightened by the rustling of a piece of paper.

When the Candidate becomes an Initiate—when he passes from the purely Mental Plane on to the Spiritual Plane—he realizes that the "I," the Real Self—is something higher than either body or mind, and that both of the latter may be used as tools and instruments by the Ego or "I." This knowledge is not reached by purely intellectual reasoning, although such efforts of the mind are often necessary to help in the unfoldment, and the Masters so use it. The real knowledge, however, comes as a special form of consciousness. The Candidate becomes "aware" of the real "I," and this consciousness being attained, he passes to the rank of the Initiates. When the Initiate passes the second degree of consciousness, and begins to grow into a realization of his relationship to the Whole—when he begins to manifest the Expansion of Self—then is he on the road to Mastership.

In the present lesson we shall endeavor to point out to the Candidate the methods of developing or increasing the realization of this "I" consciousness—this first-degree work.

We give the following exercises or development drills for the Candidate to practice. He will find that a careful and conscientious following of these directions will tend to unfold in him a sufficient degree of the "I" consciousness, to enable him to enter into higher stages of development and power. All that is necessary is for the Candidate to feel within himself the dawn of the awakening consciousness, or awareness of the Real Self. The higher stages of the "I" consciousness come gradually, for once on the Path there is no retrogression or going backward. There may be pauses on the journey, but there is no such thing as actually losing that which is once gained on The Path.

This "I" consciousness, even in its highest stages, is but a preliminary step toward what is called "Illumination," and which signifies the awakening of the Initiate to a realization of his actual connection with and relation to the Whole. The full sight of the glory of the "I," is but a faint reflected glow of "Illumination." The Candidate, once that he enters fully into the "I" consciousness, becomes an "Initiate." And the Initiate who enters into the dawn of Illumination takes his first step upon the road to Mastery. The Initiation is the awakening of the soul to a knowledge of its real existence—the Illumination is the revelation of the real nature of the soul, and of its relationship with the Whole. After the first dawn of the "I" consciousness has been attained, the Candidate is more able to grasp the means of developing the consciousness to a still higher degree—is more able to use the powers latent within him; to control his own mental states; to manifest a Centre of Consciousness and Influence that will radiate into the outer world, which is always striving and hunting for such centres around which it may revolve.

Man must master himself before he can hope to exert an

influence beyond himself. There is no royal road to unfold-ment and power—each step must be taken in turn, and each Candidate must take the step himself, and by his own effort. But he may, and will, be aided by the helping hand of the teachers who have traveled The Path before him, and who know just when that helping hand is needed to lift the Candidate over the rough places.

We bid the Candidate to pay strict attention to the following instruction, as it is all important. Do not slight any part of it, for we are giving you only what is necessary, and are stating it as briefly as possible. Pay attention, and follow the instruction closely. This lesson must be mastered before you progress. And it must be practiced not only now, but at many stages of the journey, until full Initiation and Illumination is yours.

RULES AND EXERCISES
DESIGNED TO AID THE CANDIDATE
IN HIS INITIATION

The first instruction along the line of Initiation is designed to awaken the mind to a full realization and consciousness of the individuality of the "I." The Candidate is taught to relax his body, and to calm his mind and to meditate upon the "I" until it is presented clearly and sharply before the consciousness. We herewith give directions for producing the desired physical and mental condition, in which meditation and concentration are more readily practiced. This state of Meditation will be referred to in subsequent exercises, so the Candidate is advised to acquaint himself thoroughly with it.

State of Meditation

If possible, retire to a quiet place or room, where you do not fear interruption, so that your mind may feel secure and at rest. Of course, the ideal condition cannot always be obtained, in which case you must do the best you can. The idea is that you should be able to abstract yourself, so far as is possible, from distracting impressions, and you should be alone with yourself—in communion with your Real Self.

It is well to place yourself in an easy chair, or on a couch, so that you may relax the muscles and free the tension of your nerves. You should be able to "let go" all over, allowing every muscle to become limp, until a feeling of perfect peace and restful calm permeates every particle of your being. Rest the body and calm the mind. This condition is best in the earlier stages of the practice, although after the Candidate has acquired a degree of mastery he will be able to obtain the physical relaxation and mental calm whenever and wherever he desires.

But he must guard against acquiring a "dreamy" way of going around, wrapped in meditation when he should be attending to the affairs of life. *Remember this*, the State of Meditation should be entirely under the control of the Will, and should be entered into only deliberately and at the proper times. The Will must be master of this, as well as of every other mental state. The Initiates are not "daydreamers," but men and women having full control of themselves and their moods. The "I" consciousness, while developed by meditation and consciousness, soon becomes a fixed item of consciousness, and does not have to be produced by meditation. In time of trial, doubt, or trouble, the consciousness may be brightened by an effort of the Will (as we shall explain in subsequent lessons) without going into the State of Meditation.

The Realization of the "I"

The Candidate must first acquaint himself with the reality of the "I," before he will be able to learn its real nature. This is the first step. Let the Candidate place himself in the State of Meditation, as heretofore described. Then let him concentrate his entire attention upon his Individual Self, shutting out all thought of the outside world, and other persons. Let him form in his mind the idea of himself as a *real* thing—an actual being—an individual entity—a Sun around which revolves the world. He must see himself as the Centre around which the whole world revolves. Let not a false modesty, or sense of depreciation interfere with this idea, for you are not denying the right of others to also consider themselves centres. You are, in fact, a centre of consciousness—made so by the Absolute—and you are awakening to the fact. Until the Ego recognizes itself as a Centre of Thought, Influence and Power, it will not be able to *manifest* these qualities. And in proportion as it recognizes its position as a centre, so will it be able to manifest its qualities. It is not necessary that you should compare yourself with others, or imagine yourself greater or higher than them. In fact, such comparisons are to be regretted, and are unworthy of the advanced Ego, being a mark and indication of a lack of development, rather than the reverse. In the Meditation simply ignore all consideration of the respective qualities of others, and endeavor to realize the fact that YOU are a great Centre of Consciousness—a Centre of Power—a Centre of Influence—a Centre of Thought. And that like the planets circling around the sun, so does your world revolve around YOU who are its centre.

It will not be necessary for you to argue out this matter, or to convince yourself of its truth by intellectual reasoning. The knowledge does not come in that way. It comes in the shape of a realization of the truth gradually dawning upon your consciousness through meditation and concentration. Carry this thought of yourself as a "Centre of Consciousness—Influence—Power" with you, *for it is an occult truth,* and in the proportion that you are able to realize it so will be your ability to manifest the qualities named.

No matter how humble may be your position—no matter how hard may be your lot—no matter how deficient in educational advantages you may be—still you would not change your "I" with the most fortunate, wisest and highest man or woman in the world. You may doubt this, but think for a moment and you will see that we are right. When you say that you "would like to be" this person or that, you really mean that *you* would like to have their degree of intelligence, power, wealth, position, or whatnot. What you want is something that is theirs, or something akin to it. But you would not for a moment wish to merge your *identity* with theirs, or to exchange *selves.* Think of this for a moment. To *be* the other person you would have to let *yourself* die, and instead of *yourself* you would be the other person. The real *you* would be wiped out of existence, and you would not be *you* at all, but would be *he.*

If you can but grasp this idea you will see that not for a moment would you be willing for such an exchange. Of course such an exchange is impossible. The "I" of you cannot be wiped out. It is eternal, and will go on, and on, and on, to higher and higher states—but it always will be the same "I."

Just as you, although a far different sort of person from your childhood self, still recognize that the same "I" is there, and always has been there. And although you will attain knowledge, experience, power and wisdom in the coming years, the same "I" will be there. The "I" is the Divine Spark and cannot be extinguished.

The majority of people in the present stage of the race development have but a faint conception of the reality of the "I." They accept the statement of its existence, and are conscious of themselves as an eating, sleeping, living creature—something like a higher form of animal. But they have not awakened to an "awareness" or realization of the "I," which must come to all who become real centres of Influence and Power. Some men have stumbled into this consciousness, or a degree of it, without understanding the matter. They have "felt" the truth of it, and they have stepped out from the ranks of the commonplace people of the world, and have become powers for good or bad. This is unfortunate to some extent, as this "awareness" without the knowledge that should accompany it may bring pain to the individual and others.

The Candidate must meditate upon the "I," and recognize it—*feel* it—to be a Centre. This is his first task. Impress upon your mind the word "I," in this sense and understanding, and let it sink deep down into your consciousness, so that it will become a part of you. And when you say "I," you must accompany the word with the picture of your Ego as a Centre of Consciousness, and Thought, and Power, and Influence. See yourself thus, surrounded by your world. Wherever you go, there goes the Centre of your world. YOU are the Centre, and all outside of you revolves around that Centre. This is the first great lesson on the road to Initiation. Learn it!

The Yogi Masters teach the Candidates that their realization of the "I" as a Centre may be hastened by going into the Silence, or State of Meditation, and repeating their first name over slowly, deliberately and solemnly a number of times. This exercise tends to cause the mind to centre upon the "I," and many cases of dawning Initiation have resulted from this practice. Many original thinkers have stumbled upon this method, without having been taught it. A noted example is that of Lord Tennyson, who has written that he attained a degree of Initiation in this way. He would repeat his own name, over and over, and the same time meditating upon his identity, and he reports that he would become conscious and "aware" of his reality and immortality—in short would recognize himself as a *real* center of consciousness.

We think we have given you the key to the first stage of meditation and concentration. Before passing on, let us quote from one of the old Hindu Masters. He says, regarding this matter: "When the soul sees itself as a Centre surrounded by its circumference—when the Sun knows that it is a Sun, and is surrounded by its whirling planets—then is it ready for the Wisdom and Power of the Masters."

The Knowledge
of the Independence of the "I" from the Body

Many of the Candidates find themselves prevented from a full realization of the "I" (even after they have begun to grasp it) by the confusing of the reality of the "I" with the sense of the physical body. This is a stumbling block that is easily overcome by meditation and concentration, the independence of the "I" often becoming manifest to the Candidate in a flash, upon the proper thought being used as the subject of meditation.

The exercise is given as follows: Place yourself in the State of Meditation, and think of YOURSELF—the Real "I"—as being independent of the body, but using the body as a covering and an instrument. Think of the body as you might of a suit of clothes. Realize that you are able to leave the body, and still be the same "I." Picture yourself as doing this, and looking down upon your body. Think of the body as a shell from which you may emerge without affecting your identity. Think of yourself as mastering and controlling the body that you occupy, and using it to the best advantage, making it healthy, strong and vigorous, but still being merely a shell or covering for the real "You." Think of the body as composed of atoms and cells which are constantly changing, but which are held together by the force of your Ego, and which you can improve at Will. Realize that you are merely inhabiting the body, and using it for your convenience, just as you might use a house.

In meditating further, ignore the body entirely, and place your thought upon the Real "I" that you are beginning to feel to be "you," and you will find that your identity—your "I"—is something entirely apart from the body. You may now say "my body" with a new meaning. Divorce the idea of your being a physical being, and realize that you are above body. But do not let this conception and realization cause you to ignore the body. You must regard the body as the Temple of the Spirit, and care for it, and make it a fit habitation for the "I." Do not be frightened if, during this meditation, you happen to experience the sensation of being out of the body for a few moments, and of returning to it when you are through with the exercise. The Ego is able (in the case of the advanced Initiate) of soaring above the confines of the body, but it never severs its connection at such times. It is merely as if one were to look out of the window of a room, seeing what was going on outside, and drawing in his head when he wishes. He does not leave the room, although he may place his head outside in order to observe what is happening in the street. We do not advise the Candidate to try to cultivate this sensation—but if it comes naturally during meditation, do not fear.

Realizing the Immortality and Invincibility of the Ego

While the majority accept on faith the belief in the Immortality of the Soul, yet but few are aware that it may be demonstrated by the soul itself. The Yogi Masters teach the Candidates this lesson, as follows: The Candidate places himself in the State of Meditation, or at least in a thoughtful frame of mind, and then endeavors to "imagine" himself as "dead"— that is, he tries to form a mental conception of himself as dead. This, at first thought, appears a very easy thing to imagine, but as a matter of fact it is *impossible* to do so, for the Ego refuses to entertain the proposition, and finds it impossible to imagine it. Try it for yourself. You will find that you may be able to imagine your *body* as lying still and lifeless, but the same thought finds that in so doing *You* are standing and looking at the body. So you see that *You* are not dead at all, even in imagination, although the body may be. Or, if you refuse to disentangle yourself from your body, in imagination, you may think of your body as dead but *You* who refuse to leave it are still *alive* and recognize the dead body as a thing apart from your Real Self. No matter how you may twist it

41

you *cannot* imagine yourself as dead. The Ego insists upon being *alive* in any of these thoughts, and thus finds that it has within itself the sense and assurance of Immortality. In case of sleep or stupor resulting from a blow, or from narcotics or anaesthetics, the mind is apparently blank, but the "I" is conscious of a continuity of existence. And so one may imagine himself as being in an unconscious state, or asleep, quite easily, and sees the possibility of such a state, but when it comes to imagining the "I" as dead, the mind utterly refuses to do the work. This wonderful fact that the soul carries within itself the evidence of its own immortality is a glorious thing, but one must have reached a degree of unfoldment before he is able to grasp its full significance.

The Candidate is advised to investigate the above statement for himself, by meditation and concentration, for in order that the "I" may know its true nature and possibilities, it must realize that it cannot be destroyed or killed. It must know what it is before it is able to manifest its nature. So do not leave this part of the teaching until you have mastered it. And it is well occasionally to return to it, in order that you may impress upon the mind the fact of your immortal and eternal nature. The mere glimmering of this conception of truth will give you an increased sense of strength and power, and you will find that your Self has expanded and grown, and that you are more of a power and Centre than you have heretofore realized.

The following exercises are useful in bringing about a realization of the invincibility of the Ego—its superiority to the elements.

Place yourself in the State of Meditation, and imagine the "I" as withdrawn from the body. See it passing through the tests of air, fire and water unharmed. The body being out of the way, the soul is seen to be able of passing through the air at will—of floating like a bird—of soaring—of traveling in the ether. It may be seen as able to pass through fire without harm and without sensation, for the elements affect only the physical body, not the Real "I." Likewise it may be seen as passing through water without discomfort or danger or hurt.

This meditation will give you a sense of superiority and strength, and will show you something of the nature of the real "I." It is true that you are confined in the body, and the body may be affected by the elements, but the knowledge that the Real "I" is superior to the body—superior to the elements that affect the body—and cannot be injured any more than it can be killed, is wonderful, and tends to develop the full "I" consciousness within you. For You—the Real "I"—are not body. You are Spirit. The Ego is Immortal and Invincible, and cannot be killed and harmed. When you enter into this realization and consciousness, you will feel an influx of strength and power impossible to describe. Fear will fall from you like a worn-out cloak, and you will feel that you are "born again." An understanding of this thought will show you that the things that we have been fearing cannot affect the Real "I," but must rest content with hurting the physical body. And they may be warded off from the physical body by a proper understanding and application of the Will.

In our next lesson, you will be taught how to separate the "I" from the mechanism of the mind—how you may realize your mastery of the mind, just as you now realize your independence of the body. This knowledge must be imparted to you by degrees, and you must place your feet firmly upon one round of the ladder before you take the next step.

The watchword of this First Lesson is "I." And the Candidate must enter fully into its meaning before he is able to progress. He must realize his real existence—independent of the body. He must see himself as invincible and impervious to harm, hurt, or death. He must see himself as a great Centre of Consciousness—a Sun around which his world revolves. Then will come to him a new strength. He will feel a calm dignity and power, which will be apparent to those with whom he comes in contact. He will be able to look the world in the face without flinching, and without fear, for he will realize the nature and power of the "I." He will realize that he is a Centre of Power—of Influence. He will realize that nothing can harm the "I," and that no matter how the storms of life may dash upon the personality, the real "I"—the Individuality—is unharmed. Like a rock that stands steadfast throughout the storm, so does the "I" stand through the tempests of the life of personality. And he will know that as he grows in realization, he will be able to control these storms and bid them be still.

In the words of one of the Yogi Masters: "The 'I' is eternal. It passes unharmed through the fire, the air, the water. Sword and spear cannot kill or wound it. It cannot die. The trials of the physical life are but as dreams to it. Resting secure in the knowledge of the 'I,' Man may smile at the worst the world has to offer, and raising his hand he may bid them disappear into the mist from which they emerged. Blessed is he who can say (understandingly) 'I.'"

So dear Candidate, we leave you to master the First Lesson. Be not discouraged if your progress be slow. Be not cast down if you slip back a step after having gained it. You will gain two at the next step. Success and realization will be yours. Mastery is before. You will Attain. You will Accomplish. Peace be with you.

FIRST LESSON—MANTRAM

"I" am a Centre. Around me revolves my world.

"I" am a Centre of Influence and Power.

"I" am a Centre of Thought and Consciousness.

"I" am Independent of the Body.

"I" am Immortal and cannot be Destroyed.

"I" am Invincible and cannot be Injured.

The Ego's Mental Tools

In the First Lesson we gave instruction and exercises designed to awaken the consciousness of the Candidate to a realization of the real "I." We confined our instructions to the preliminary teachings of the reality of the "I," and the means whereby the Candidate might be brought to a realization of his real Self, and its independence from the body and the things of the flesh. We tried to show you how you might awaken to a consciousness of the reality of the "I"; its real nature; its independence of the body; its immortality; its invincibility and invulnerability. How well we have succeeded may be determined only by the experience of each Candidate, for we can but point out the way, and the Candidate must do the real work himself.

But there is more to be said and done in this matter of awakening to a realization of the "I." So far, we have but told you how to distinguish between the material coverings of the Ego and the "I" itself. We have tried to show you that you had a real "I," and then to show you what it was, and how it was independent of the material coverings, etc. But there is still another step in this self-analysis—a more difficult step. Even when the Candidate has awakened to a realization of his independence of the body, and material coverings, he often confounds the "I" with the lower principles of the mind. This is a mistake. The Mind, in its various phases and planes, is but a tool and instrument of the "I," and is far from being the "I" itself. We shall try to bring out this fact in this lesson and its accompanying exercises. We shall avoid, and pass by, the metaphysical features of the case, and shall confine ourselves to the Yogi Psychology. We shall not touch upon theories, nor attempt to explain the cause, nature and purpose of the Mind—the working tool of the Ego—but instead shall attempt to point out a way whereby you may analyze the Mind and then determine which is the "not I" and which is the real "I." It is useless to burden you with theories or metaphysical talk, when the way to prove the thing is right within your own grasp. By using the mind, you will be able to separate it into its parts, and force it to give you its own answer to the questions touching itself.

In the second and third lessons of our *Fourteen Lessons,* we pointed out to you the fact that man had three Mental Principles, or subdivisions of mind, all of which were below the plane of Spirit. The "I" is Spirit, but its mental principles are of a lower order. Without wishing to unduly repeat ourselves, we think it better to run hastily over these three Principles in the mind of Man.

First, there is what is known as the Instinctive Mind, which man shares in common with the lower animals. It is the first principle of mind that appears in the scale of evolution. In its lowest phases, consciousness is but barely perceptible, and mere sensation is apparent. In its higher stages it almost reaches the plane of Reason or Intellect, in fact, they overlap each other, or, rather, blend into each other. The Instinctive Mind does valuable work in the direction of maintaining animal life in our bodies, it having charge of this part of our being. It attends to the constant work of repair; replacement; change; digestion; assimilation; elimination, etc., all of which work is performed below the plane of consciousness.

But this is but a small part of the work of the Instinctive Mind. For this part of the mind has stored up all the experiences of ourselves and ancestors in our evolution from the lower forms of animal life into the present stage of evolution. All of the old animal instincts (which were all right in their place, and quite necessary for the well-being of the lower forms of life) have left traces in this part of the mind, which traces are apt to come to the front under pressure of unusual circumstances, even long after we think we have outgrown them. In this part of the mind are to be found traces of the old fighting instinct of the animal; all the animal passions; all the hate, envy, jealousy, and the rest of it, which are our inheritances from the past. The Instinctive Mind is also the "habit mind" in which is stored up all the little, and great, habits of many lives, or rather such as have not been entirely effaced by subsequent habits of a stronger nature. The Instinctive Mind is a queer storehouse, containing quite a variety of objects, many of them very good in their way, but others of which are the worst kind of old junk and rubbish.

This part of the mind also is the seat of the appetites; passions; desires; instincts; sensations; feelings and emotions of the lower order, manifested in the lower animals; primitive man; the barbarian; and the man of today, the difference being only in the degree of control over them that has been gained by the higher parts of the mind. There are higher desires, aspirations, etc., belonging to a higher part of the mind, which we will describe in a few minutes, but the "animal nature" belongs to the Instinctive Mind. To it also belong the "feelings" belonging to our emotional and passional nature. All animal desires, such as hunger and thirst; sexual desires (on the physical plane); all passions, such as physical love; hatred; envy; malice; jealousy; revenge, etc., are part of this part of the mind. The desire for the physical (unless a means of reaching higher things) and the longing for the material, belong to this region of the mind. The "lust of the flesh; the lust of the eyes; the pride of life," belong to the Instinctive Mind.

Take note, however, that we are not condemning the things belonging to this plane of the mind. All of them have their place—many were necessary in the past, and many are still necessary for the continuance of physical life. All are right in their place, and to those in the particular plane of development to which they belong, and are wrong only when one is mastered by them, or when he returns to pick up an unworthy thing that has been cast off in the unfoldment of the individual. This lesson has nothing to do with the right and wrong of these things (we have treated of that elsewhere) and we mention this part of the mind that you may understand that you have such a thing in your mental makeup, and that you may understand the thought, etc., coming from it, when we start in to analyze the mind in the latter part of this lesson. All we will ask you to do at this stage of the lesson is to realize that this part of the mind, while *belonging* to you, is *not* You, yourself. It is *not* the "I" part of you.

Next in order, above the Instinctive Mind, is what we

have called the Intellect, that part of the mind that does our reasoning, analyzing; "thinking," etc. You are using it in the consideration of this lesson. But note this: You are *using* it, but it is *not* You, any more than was the Instinctive Mind that you considered a moment ago. You will begin to make the separation, if you will think but a moment. We will not take up your time with a consideration of Intellect or Reason. You will find a good description of this part of the mind in any good elementary work on Psychology. Our only idea in mentioning it is that you may make the classification, and that we may afterward show you that the Intellect is but a tool of the Ego, instead of being the real "I" itself, as so many seem to imagine.

The third, and highest, Mental Principle is what is called the Spiritual Mind, that part of the mind which is almost unknown to many of the race, but which has developed into consciousness with nearly all who read this lesson, for the fact that the subject of this lesson attracts you is a proof that this part of your mental nature is unfolding into consciousness. This region of the mind is the source of that which we call "genius," "inspiration," "spirituality," and all that we consider the "highest" in our mental makeup. All the great thoughts and ideas float into the field of consciousness from this part of the mind. All the great unfoldment of the race comes from there. All the higher mental ideas that have come to Man in his upward evolutionary journey, that tend in the direction of nobility; true religious feeling; kindness; humanity; justice; unselfish love; mercy; sympathy, etc., have come to him through his slowly unfolding Spiritual Mind. His love of God and of his fellow man have come in this way. His knowledge of the great occult truths reach him through this channel. The mental realization of the "I," which we are

51

endeavoring to teach in these lessons, must come to him by way of the Spiritual Mind unfolding its ideas into his field of consciousness.

But even this great and wonderful part of the mind is but a tool—a highly finished one, it is true, but still a tool—to the Ego, or "I."

We propose to give you a little mental drill work, toward the end that you may be able more readily to distinguish the "I" from the mind, or mental states. In this connection we would say that every part, plane, and function of the mind is good, and necessary, and the student must not fall into the error of supposing that because we tell him to set aside first this part of the mind and then that part, that we are undervaluing the mind, or that we regard it as an encumbrance or hindrance. Far from this, we realize that it is *by the use of* the mind that Man is enabled to arrive at a knowledge of his true nature and Self, and that his progress through many stages yet will depend upon the unfolding of his mental faculties.

Man is now using but the lower and inferior parts of his mind, and he has within his mental world great unexplored regions that far surpass anything of which the human mind has dreamed. In fact, it is part of the business of Raja Yoga to aid in unfolding these higher faculties and mental regions. And so far from decrying the Mind, the Raja Yoga teachers are chiefly concerned in recognizing the Mind's power and possibilities, and directing the student to avail himself of the latent powers that are inherent in his soul.

It is only by the mind that the teachings we are now giving you may be grasped and understood, and used to your advantage and benefit. We are talking direct to your mind now, and are making appeals to it, that it may be interested and may open itself to what is ready to come into it from its own higher regions. We are appealing to the Intellect to direct its attention to this great matter, that it may interpose less resistance to the truths that are waiting to be projected from the Spiritual Mind, which knows the Truth.

MENTAL DRILL

Place yourself in a calm, restful condition, that you may be able to meditate upon the matters that we shall place before you for consideration. Allow the matters presented to meet with a hospitable reception from you, and hold a mental attitude of willingness to receive what may be waiting for you in the higher regions of your mind.

We wish to call your attention to several mental impressions or conditions, one after another, in order that you may realize that they are merely something *incident* to you, and *not* YOU yourself—that you may set them aside and consider them, just as you might anything that you have been using. You cannot set the "I" aside and so consider it, but the various forms of the "not I" may be so set aside and considered.

In the First Lesson you gained the perception of the "I" as independent from the body, the latter merely being an instrument for use. You have now arrived at the stage when the "I" appears to you to be a mental creature—a bundle of thoughts, feelings, moods, etc. But you must go further. You must be able to distinguish the "I" from these mental conditions, which are as much tools as is the body and its parts.

Let us begin by considering the thoughts more closely connected with the body, and then work up to the higher mental states.

The sensations of the body, such as hunger; thirst;

53

pain; pleasurable sensations; physical desires, etc., etc., are not apt to be mistaken for essential qualities of the "I" by many of the Candidates, for they have passed beyond this stage, and have learned to set aside these sensations, to a greater or lesser extent, by an effort of the Will, and are no longer slaves to them. Not that they do not experience these sensations, but they have grown to regard them as incidents of the physical life—good in their place—but useful to the advanced man only when he has mastered them to the extent that he no longer regards them as close to the "I." And yet, to some people, these sensations are so closely identified with their conception of the "I" that when they think of themselves they think merely of a bundle of these sensations. They are not able to set them aside and consider them as things apart, to be used when necessary and proper, but as things not fastened to the "I." The more advanced a man becomes the farther off seem these sensations. Not that he does not feel hungry, for instance. Not at all, for he recognizes hunger, and satisfies it within reason, knowing that his physical body is making demands for attention, and that these demands should be heeded. But—mark the difference—instead of feeling that the *"I"* is hungry the man feels that *"my body"* is hungry, just as he might become conscious that his horse or dog was crying for food insistently. Do you see what we mean? It is that the man no longer identifies himself—the "I"—with the body, consequently the thoughts which are most closely allied to the physical life seem comparatively "separate" from his "I" conception. Such a man thinks "my stomach, this," or "my leg, that," or "my body, thus," instead of "'I,' this," or "'I' that." He is able, almost automatically, to think of the body and its sensations as things *of* him, and *belonging to* him, which require attention and care, rather than as real parts of the "I." He is able to form a conception of the "I" as existing without any of these things—without the body and its sensations—and so he has taken the first step in the realization of the "I."

Before going on, we ask the students to stop a few moments, and mentally run over these sensations of the body. Form a mental image of them, and realize that they are merely incidents to the present stage of growth and experience of the "I," and that they form no real part of it. They may, and will be, left behind in the Ego's higher planes of advancement. You may have attained this mental conception perfectly, long since, but we ask that to give yourself the mental drill at this time, in order to fasten upon your mind this first step.

In realizing that you are able to set aside, mentally, these sensations—that you are able to hold them out at arm's length and "consider" them as an "outside" thing, you mentally determine that they are "not I" things, and you set them down in the "not I" collection—the first to be placed there. Let us try to make this still plainer, even at the risk of wearying you by repetitions (for you must get this idea firmly fixed in your mind). To be able to say that a thing is "not I," you must realize that there are two things in question: (1) the "not I" thing, and (2) the "I" who is regarding the "not I" thing just as the "I" regards a lump of sugar, or a mountain. Do you see what we mean? Keep at it until you do.

Next, consider some of the emotions, such as anger; hate; love, in its ordinary forms; jealousy; ambition; and the hundred and one other emotions that sweep through our brains. You will find that you are able to set each one of these emotions or feelings aside and study it; dissect it; analyze it; consider it. You will be able to understand the rise, progress and end of each of these feelings, as they have come to you, and as you recall them in your memory or imagination, just as readily as you would were you observing their occurrence in the mind of a friend. You will find them all stored away in some parts of your mental makeup, and you may (to use a modern American slang phrase) "make them trot before you, and show their paces." Don't you see that they are not "You"—that they are merely something that you carry around with you in a mental bag. You can imagine yourself as living without them, and still being "I," can you not?

And the very fact that you are able to set them aside and examine and consider them is a proof that they are "not I" things—for there are two things in the matter: (1) *You* who are examining and considering them, and (2) the thing itself which is the *object* of the examination and consideration at mental arm's length. So into the "not I" collection go these emotions, desirable and undesirable. The collection is steadily growing, and will attain quite formidable proportions after a while.

Now, do not imagine that this is a lesson designed to teach you how to discard these emotions, although if it enables you to get rid of the undesirable ones, so much the better. This is not our object, for we bid you place the desirable (at this time) ones in with the opposite kind, the idea being to bring you to a realization that the "I" is higher, above and independent of these mental somethings, and then when you have realized the nature of the "I," you may return and use (as a Master) the things that have been using you as a slave. So do not be afraid to throw these emotions (good and bad) into the "not I" collection. You may go back to them, and use the good ones, after the Mental Drill is over. No matter how much you may think that you are

56

bound by any of these emotions, you will realize, by careful analysis, that it is of the "not I" kind, for the "I" existed before the emotion came into active play, and it will live long after the emotion has faded away. The principal proof is that you are able to hold it out at arm's length and examine it—a proof that it is "not I."

Run through the entire list of your feelings; emotions; moods; and whatnot, just as you would those of a well-known friend or relative, and you will see that each one—every one—is a "not I" thing, and you will lay it aside for the time, for the purpose of the scientific experiment, at least.

Then passing on to the Intellect, you will be able to hold out for examination each mental process and principle. You don't believe it, you may say. Then read and study some good work on Psychology, and you will learn to dissect and analyze every intellectual process—and to classify it and place it in the proper pigeonhole. Study Psychology by means of some good textbook, and you will find that one by one every intellectual process is classified, and talked about and labeled, just as you would a collection of flowers. If that does not satisfy you, turn the leaves of some work on Logic, and you will admit that you may hold these intellectual processes at arm's length and examine them, and talk about them to others. So that these wonderful tools of Man—the Intellectual powers may be placed in the "not I" collection, for the "I" is capable of standing aside and viewing them—it is able to detach them from itself. The most remarkable thing about this is that in admitting this fact, you realize that the "I" is using these very intellectual faculties to pass upon themselves. Who is the Master that compels these faculties to do this to themselves? The Master of the Mind—The "I."

And reaching the higher regions of the mind—even

the Spiritual Mind, you will be compelled to admit that the things that have come into consciousness from that region may be considered and studied, just as may be any other mental thing, and so even these high things must be placed in the "not I" collection. You may object that this does not prove that all the things in the Spiritual Mind may be so treated—that there may be "I" things there that cannot be so treated. We will not discuss this question, for you know nothing about the Spiritual Mind except as it has revealed itself to you, and the higher regions of that mind are like the mind of a God, when compared to what *you* call mind. But the evidence of the Illumined—those in whom the Spiritual Mind has wonderfully unfolded tell us that even in the highest forms of development, the Initiates, yea, even the Masters, realize that above even their highest mental states there is always that eternal "I" brooding over them, as the Sun over the lake; and that the highest conception of the "I" known even to advanced souls, is but a faint reflection of the "I" filtering through the Spiritual Mind, although that Spiritual Mind is as clear as the clearest crystal when compared with our comparatively opaque mental states. And the highest mental state is but a tool or instrument of the "I," and is not the "I" itself.

And yet the "I" is to be found in the faintest forms of consciousness, and animates even the unconscious life. The "I" is always the same, but its apparent growth is the result of the mental unfoldment of the individual. As we described it in one of the lessons of the *Advanced Course* it is like an electric lamp that is encased in many wrappings of cloth. As cloth after cloth is removed, the light seems to grow brighter and stronger, and yet it has changed not, the change being in the removal of the confining and bedimming coverings. We do not expect to make you realize the "I" in all its fullness—

58

that is far beyond the highest known to man of today—but we do hope to bring you to a realization of the highest conception of the "I," possible to each of you in your present stage of unfoldment, and in the process we expect to cause to drop from you some of the confining sheaths that you have about outgrown. The sheaths are ready for dropping, and all that is required is the touch of a friendly hand to cause them to fall fluttering from you. We wish to bring you to the fullest possible (to you) realization of the "I," in order to make an Individual of you—in order that you may understand, and have courage to take up the tools and instruments lying at your hand, and do the work before you.

And now, back to the Mental Drill. After you have satisfied yourself that most everything that you are capable of thinking about is a "not I" thing—a tool and instrument for your use—you will ask, "And now, what is there left that should not be thrown in the "not I" collection?" To this question we answer "THE 'I' ITSELF." And when you demand a proof we say, "Try to set aside the 'I' for consideration!" You may try from now until the passing away of infinities of infinities, and you will never be able to set aside the real "I" for consideration. You may think you can, but a little reflection will show you that you are merely setting aside some of your mental qualities or faculties. And in this process what is the "I" doing? Simply setting aside and considering things. Can you not see that the "I" cannot be both the *considerer* and the thing considered—the *examiner* and the thing examined? Can the sun shine upon itself by its own light? You may consider the "I" of some other person, but it is *your* "I" that is considering. But you cannot, as an "I," stand aside and see yourself as an "I." Then what evidence have we that there is an "I" to us? This: that you are always conscious of being the

considerer and examiner, instead of the considered and examined thing—and then, you have the evidence of your consciousness. And what report does this consciousness give us?
Simply this, and nothing more: "I AM." That is all that the "I"
is conscious of, regarding its true self: "I AM," but that consciousness is worth all the rest, for the rest is but "not I" tools
that the "I" may reach out and use.

And so at the final analysis, you will find that there is
something that refuses to be set aside and examined by the
"I." And that something is the "I" itself—that "I" eternal, unchangeable—that drop of the Great Spirit Ocean—that spark
from the Sacred Flame.

Just as you find it impossible to imagine the "I" as dead,
so will you find it impossible to set aside the "I" for consideration—all that comes to you is the testimony: "I AM."

If you were able to set aside the "I" for consideration,
who would be the one to consider it? Who could consider
except the "I" itself, and if it be *here*, how could it be *there*?
The "I" cannot be the "not I" even in the wildest flights of the
imagination—the imagination with all its boasted freedom
and power, confesses itself vanquished when asked to do this
thing.

Oh, students, may you be brought to a realization of
what you are. May you soon awaken to the fact that you are
sleeping gods—that you have within you the power of the
Universe, awaiting your word to manifest in action. Long ages
have you toiled to get this far, and long must you travel before you reach even the first Great Temple, but you are now
entering into the conscious stage of Spiritual Evolution. No
longer will your eyes be closed as you walk the Path. From
now on you will begin to see clearer and clearer each step, in
the dawning light of consciousness.

You are in touch with all of life, and the separation of your "I" from the great Universal "I" is but apparent and temporary. We will tell you of these things in our Third Lesson, but before you can grasp that you must develop the "I" consciousness within you. Do not lay aside this matter as one of no importance. Do not dismiss our weak explanation as being "merely words, words, words," as so many are inclined to do. We are pointing out a great truth to you. Why not follow the leadings of the Spirit which even now—this moment while you read—is urging you to walk The Path of Attainment? Consider the teachings of this lesson, and practice the Mental Drill until your mind has grasped its significance, then let it sink deep down into your inner consciousness. Then will you be ready for the next lessons, and those to follow.

Practice this Mental Drill until you are fully assured of the *reality* of the "I" and the *relativity* of the "not "I"" in the mind. When you once grasp this truth, you will find that you will be able to use the mind with far greater power and effect, for you will recognize that it is your tool and instrument, fitted and intended to do your bidding. You will be able to master your moods, and emotions when necessary, and will rise from the position of a slave to a Master.

Our words seem cheap and poor, when we consider the greatness of the truth that we are endeavoring to convey by means of them. For who can find words to express the inexpressible? All that we may hope to do is to awaken a keen interest and attention on your part, so that you will practice the Mental Drill, and thus obtain the evidence of your own mentality to the truth. Truth is not truth to you until you have proven it in your own experience, and once so proven you cannot be robbed of it, nor can it be argued away from you.

You must realize that in every mental effort You—the "I"—are behind it. You bid the Mind work, and it obeys your Will. You are the Master, and not the slave of your mind. You are the Driver, not the driven. Shake yourself loose from the tyranny of the mind that has oppressed you for so long. Assert yourself, and be free. We will help you in this direction during the course of these lessons, but you must first assert yourself as a Master of your Mind. Sign the mental Declaration of Independence from your moods, emotions, and uncontrolled thoughts, and assert your Dominion over them. Enter into your Kingdom, thou manifestation of the Spirit!

While this lesson is intended primarily to bring clearly into your consciousness the fact that the "I" is a reality, separate and distinct from its Mental Tools, and while the control of the mental faculties by the Will forms a part of some of the future lessons, still, we think that this is a good place to point out to you the advantages arising from a realization of the true nature of the "I" and the relative aspect of the Mind.

Many of us have supposed that our minds were the masters of ourselves, and we have allowed ourselves to be tormented and worried by thoughts "running away" with us, and presenting themselves at inopportune moments. The Initiate is relieved from this annoyance, for he learns to assert his mastery over the different parts of the mind, and controls and regulates his mental processes, just as one would a fine piece of machinery. He is able to control his conscious thinking faculties, and direct their work to the best advantage, and he also learns how to pass on orders to the subconscious mental region and bid it work for him while he sleeps, or even when he is using his conscious mind in other matters. These subjects will be considered by us in due time, during the course of lessons.

In this connection it may be interesting to read what Edward Carpenter[2] says of the power of the individual to control his thought processes. In his book *From Adam's Peak to Elephanta*, in describing his experience while visiting a Hindu Gnani Yogi, he says:

> And if we are unwilling to believe in this internal mastery over the body, we are perhaps almost equally unaccustomed to the idea of mastery over our own inner thoughts and feelings. That a man should be a prey to any thought that chances to take possession of his mind, is commonly among us assumed as unavoidable. It may be a matter of regret that he should be kept awake all night from anxiety as to the issue of a lawsuit on the morrow, but that he should have the power of determining whether he be kept awake or not seems an extravagant demand. The image of an impending calamity is no doubt odious, but its very odiousness (we say) makes it haunt the mind all the more pertinaciously and it is useless to try to expel it.
>
> Yet this is an absurd position—for man, the heir of all the ages: hag-ridden by the flimsy creatures of his own brain. If a pebble in our boot torments us, we expel it. We take off the boot and shake it out. And once the matter is fairly understood it is just as easy to expel an intruding and obnoxious thought from the mind. About this there ought to be no mistake, no two opinions. The thing is obvious, clear and unmistakable. It should be as easy to expel an obnoxious thought from your mind as it is to shake a stone out of your shoe; and till a man can do that it is just nonsense to talk about his ascendancy over Nature, and all the rest of it. He is a mere slave, and prey to the bat-winged phantoms that flit through the corridors of his own brain.

Yet the weary and careworn faces that we meet by thousands, even among the affluent classes of civilization, testify only too clearly how seldom this mastery is obtained. How rare indeed to meet a *man!* How common rather to discover a creature hounded on by tyrant thoughts (or cares or desires), cowering, wincing under the lash—or perchance priding himself to run merrily in obedience to a driver that rattles the reins and persuades him that he is free—whom we cannot converse with in careless *tete-a-tete* because that alien presence is always there, on the watch.

It is one of the most prominent doctrines of Raja Yoga that the power of expelling thoughts, or if need be, killing them dead on the spot, *must* be attained. Naturally the art requires practice, but like other arts, when once acquired there is no mystery or difficulty about it. And it is worth practice. It may indeed fairly be said that life only begins when this art has been acquired. For obviously when instead of being ruled by individual thoughts, the whole flock of them in their immense multitude and variety and capacity is ours to direct and dispatch and employ where we list ('for He maketh the winds his messengers and the flaming fire His minister'), life becomes a thing so vast and grand compared with what it was before, that its former condition may well appear almost antenatal.

If you can kill a thought dead, for the time being, you can do anything else with it that you please. And therefore it is that this power is so valuable. And it not only frees a man from mental torment (which is nine-tenths at least of the torment of life), but it gives him a concentrated power of handling mental work absolutely unknown to him before. The two things are correlative to each other. As already said this is one of the principles of Raja Yoga.

While at work your thought is to be absolutely concentrated in it, undistracted by anything whatever irrelevant to the matter in hand—pounding away like a great engine, with giant power and perfect economy—no wear and tear of friction, or dislocation of parts owing to the working of different forces at the same time. Then when the work is finished, if there is no more occasion for the use of the machine, it must stop equally, absolutely—stop entirely—no *worrying* (as if a parcel of boys were allowed to play their devilments with a locomotive as soon as it was in the shed)—and the man must retire into that region of his consciousness where his true self dwells.

I say the power of the thought-machine itself is enormously increased by this faculty of letting it alone on the one hand, and of using it singly and with concentration on the other. It becomes a true tool, which a master workman lays down when done with, but which only a bungler carries about with him all the time to show that he is the possessor of it.

We ask the students to read carefully the above quotations from Mr. Carpenter's book, for they are full of suggestions that may be taken up to advantage by those who are emancipating themselves from their slavery to the unmastered mind, and who are now bringing the mind under control of the Ego, by means of the Will.

Our next lesson will take up the subject of the relationship of the "I" to the Universal "I," and will be called the "Expansion of the Self." It will deal with the subject, not from a theoretical standpoint, but from the position of the teacher who is endeavoring to make his students actually *aware* in their consciousness of the truth of the proposition. In this course we are not trying to make our students past-masters of *theory*, but are endeavoring to place them in a position whereby they may *know* for themselves, and actually experience the things of which we teach.

Therefore we urge upon you not to merely rest content with reading this lesson, but, instead, to study and meditate upon the teachings mentioned under the head of "Mental Drill," until the distinctions stand out clearly in your mind, and until you not only *believe* them to be true, but actually are *conscious* of the "I" and its Mental Tools. Have patience and perseverance. The task may be difficult, but the reward is great. To become conscious of the greatness, majesty, strength and power of your real being is worth years of hard study. Do you not think so? Then study and practice hopefully, diligently and earnestly.

Peace be with you.

SECOND LESSON—MANTRAM

"I" am an entity—my mind is my
instrument of expression.

"I" exist independent of my mind, and am not
dependent upon it for existence or being.

"I" am Master of my mind, not its slave.

"I" can set aside my sensations, emotions,
passions, desires, intellectual faculties, and all
the rest of my mental collection of tools, as "not I"
things—and still there remains something—and that
something is "I," which cannot be set aside by me,
for it is my very self; my only self; my real self—"I."
That which remains after all that may be set aside
is set aside is the "I"—Myself—eternal, constant,
unchangeable.

The Expansion of the Self

In the first two lessons of this course we have endeavored to bring to the candidate a realization in consciousness of the reality of the "I," and to enable him to distinguish between the Self and its sheaths, physical and mental. In the present lesson we will call his attention to the relationship of the "I" to the Universal "I," and will endeavor to give him an idea of a greater, grander Self, transcending personality and the little self that we are so apt to regard as the "I."

The keynote of this lesson will be "The Oneness of All," and all of its teachings will be directed to awakening a realization in consciousness of that great truth. But we wish to impress upon the mind of the Candidate that we are *not* teaching him that he is the Absolute. We are not teaching the "I Am God" belief, which we consider to be erroneous and misleading, and a perversion of the original Yogi teachings. This false teaching has taken possession of many of the Hindu teachers and people, and with its accompanying teaching of *Maya* or the complete illusion or nonexistence of the Universe, has reduced millions of people to a passive, negative mental condition which undoubtedly is retarding their progress. Not only in India is this true, but the same facts may be observed among the pupils of the Western teachers who have embraced this negative side of the Oriental Philosophy. Such people confound the "Absolute" and "Relative" aspects of the One, and, being unable to reconcile the facts of Life and the Universe with their theories of "I Am God," they are driven to the desperate expedient of boldly denying the Universe, and declaring it to be all an illusion or Maya.

You will have no trouble in distinguishing the pupils of the teachers holding this view. They will be found to exhibit the most negative mental condition—a natural result of absorbing the constant suggestion of "nothingness"—the gospel of negation. In marked contrast to the mental condition of the students, however, will be observed the mental attitude of the teachers, who are almost uniformly examples of vital, positive, mental force, capable of hurling their teaching into the minds of the pupils—of driving in their statements by the force of an awakened Will. The teacher, as a rule, has awakened to a sense of the "I" consciousness, and really develops the same by his "I Am God" attitude, because by holding this mental attitude he is enabled to throw off the influence of the sheaths of the lower mental principles, and the light of the Self shows forth fiercely and strongly, sometimes to such an extent that it fairly scorches the mentality of the less advanced pupil. But, notwithstanding this awakened "I" consciousness, the teacher is handicapped by his intellectual misconception and befogging metaphysics, and is unable to impart the "I" consciousness to his pupils, and, instead of raising them up to shine with equal splendor with himself, he really forces them into a shadow by reason of his teachings.

Our students, of course, will understand that the above is not written in the spirit of carping criticism or faultfinding. We hold no such mental attitude, and indeed could not if we remain true to our conception of Truth. We are mentioning these matters simply that the student may avoid this "I Am God" pitfall which awaits the Candidate just as he has well started on the Path. It would not be such a serious matter if it were merely a question of faulty metaphysics, for that would straighten itself out in time. But it is far more serious than this, for the teaching inevitably leads to the accompanying teaching that all is Illusion or *Maya*, and that Life is but a dream—a false thing—a lie—a nightmare; that the journey along the Path is but an illusion; that everything is "nothing"; that there is no soul; that You are God in disguise, and that He is fooling Himself in making believe that He is You; that Life is but a Divine masquerade or sleight-of-hand performance; that You are God, but that You (God) are fooling Yourself (God) in order to amuse Yourself (God). Is not this horrible? And yet it shows to what lengths the human mind will go before it will part with some pet theory of metaphysics with which it has been hypnotized. Do you think that we have overdrawn the picture? Then read some of the teachings of these schools of the Oriental Philosophy, or listen to some of the more radical of the Western teachers preaching this philosophy. The majority of the latter lack the courage of the Hindu teachers in carrying their theories to a logical conclusion, and, consequently they veil their teachings with metaphysical subtlety. But a few of them are more courageous, and come out into the open and preach their doctrine in full.

Some of the modern Western teachers of this philosophy explain matters by saying that "God is masquerading as different forms of life, including Man, in order that he may gain the experience resulting therefrom, for although He has Infinite and Absolute Wisdom and Knowledge, he lacks the experience that comes only from actually living the life of the lowly forms, and therefore He descends thus in order to gain the needed experience." Can you imagine the Absolute, possessed of all possible Knowledge and Wisdom, feeling the need of such petty "experience," and living the life of the lowly forms (including Man) in order "to gain experience"? To what depths do these vain theories of Man drive us? Another leading Western teacher, who has absorbed the teaching of certain branches of the Oriental Philosophy, and who possesses the courage of his convictions, boldly announces that "You, yourself, are the *totality* of being, and with your mind alone create, preserve and destroy the universe, which is your own mental product." And again the last mentioned teacher states: "the entire universe is a bagatelle illustration of your own creative power, which you are now exhibiting for your own inspection." "By their fruits shall you know them," is a safe rule to apply to all teachings. The philosophy that teaches that the Universe is an illusion perpetrated by you (God) to amuse, entertain or fool yourself (God), can have but one result, and that is the conclusion that "everything is nothing," and all that is necessary to do is to sit down, fold your hands and enjoy the Divine exhibition of legerdemain that you are performing for your own entertainment, and then, when the show is over, return to your state of conscious Godhood and recall with smiles the pleasant memories of the "conjure show" that you created to fool yourself with during several billions of ages. That is what it amounts to, and the result is that those accepting this philosophy thrust upon them by forceful teachers, and knowing in their hearts that they are *not* God, but absorbing the suggestions of "nothingness," are driven into a state of mental apathy and negativity, the soul sinking into a stupor from which it may not be roused for a long period of time.

We wish you to avoid confounding our teaching with this just mentioned. We wish to teach you that You are a real Being—*not* God Himself, but a manifestation of Him who is the Absolute. You are a Child of the Absolute, if you prefer the term, possessed of the Divine Heritage, and whose mission it is to unfold qualities which are your inheritances from your Parent. Do not make the great mistake of confounding the Relative with the Absolute. Avoid this pitfall into which so many have fallen. Do not allow yourself to fall into the "Slough of Despond," and wallow in the mud of "nothingness," and to see no reality except in the person of some forceful teacher who takes the place of the Absolute in your mind. But raise your head and assert your Divine Parentage, and your Heritage from the Absolute, and step out boldly on the Path, asserting the "I."

(We must refer the Candidate back to our *Advanced Course*, for our teachings regarding the Absolute and the Relative. The last three lessons of that course will throw light upon what we have just said. To repeat the teaching at this point would be to use space which is needed for the lesson before us.)

And yet, while the "I" is *not* God, the Absolute, it is infinitely greater than we have imagined it to be before the light dawned upon us. It extends itself far beyond what we had conceived to be its limits. It touches the Universe at all its points, and is in the closest union with all of Life. It is in the closest touch with all that has emanated from the Absolute—all the world of Relativity. And while it faces the Relative Universe, it has its roots in the Absolute, and draws nourishment therefrom, just as does the babe in the womb obtain nourishment from the mother. It is verily a manifestation of God, and God's very essence is in it. Surely this is almost as "high" a statement as the "I Am God" of the teachers just mentioned—and yet how different. Let us consider the teaching in detail in this lesson, and in portions of others to follow.

Let us begin with a consideration of the instruments of the Ego, and the material with which and through which the Ego works. Let us realize that the physical body of man is identical in substance with all other forms of matter, and that its atoms are continually changing and being replaced, the material being drawn from the great storehouse of matter, and that there is a Oneness of matter underlying all apparent differences of form and substance. And then let us realize that the vital energy or *Prana* that man uses in his life work is but a portion of that great universal energy which permeates everything and everywhere, the portion being used by us at any particular moment being drawn from the universal supply, and again passing out from us into the great ocean of force or energy. And then let us realize that even the mind, which is so close to the real Self that it is often mistaken for it—even that wonderful thing Thought—is but a portion of the Universal Mind, the highest emanation of the Absolute beneath the plane of Spirit, and that the Mind-substance or *Chitta* that we are using this moment, is not ours separately and distinctly, but is simply a portion from the great universal supply, which is constant and unchangeable. Let us then realize that even this thing that we feel pulsing within us—

74

that which is so closely bound up with the Spirit as to be almost inseparable from it—that which we call Life—is but a bit of that Great Life Principle that pervades the Universe, and which cannot be added to, nor subtracted from. When we have realized these things, and have begun to feel our relation (in these particulars) to the One Great Emanation of the Absolute, then we may begin to grasp the idea of the Oneness of Spirit, and the relation of the "I" to every other "I," and the merging of the Self into the one great Self, which is not the extinction of Individuality, as some have supposed, but the enlargement and extension of the Individual Consciousness until it takes in the Whole.

In Lessons X and XI of the *Advanced Course* we called your attention to the Yogi teachings concerning *Akasa* or Matter, and showed you that all forms of what we know as Matter are but different forms of manifestation of the principle called *Akasa*, or as the Western scientists call it, "Ether." This Ether or *Akasa* is the finest, thinnest and most tenuous form of Matter, in fact it is Matter in its ultimate or fundamental form, the different forms of what we call Matter being but manifestations of this *Akasa* or Ether, the apparent difference resulting from different rates of vibration, etc. We mention this fact here merely to bring clearly before your mind the fact of the Universality of Matter, to the end that you may realize that each and every particle of your physical body is but a portion of this great principle of the Universe, fresh from the great storehouse, and just about returning to it again, for the atoms of the body are constantly changing. That which appears as your flesh today, may have been part of a plant a few days before, and may be part of some other living thing a few days hence. Constant change is going on, and what is yours today was someone's else yesterday, and still another's tomorrow. You do not own one atom of matter *personally*, it is all a part of the common supply, the stream flowing through you and through all Life, on and on forever.

And so it is with the Vital Energy that you are using every moment of your life. You are constantly drawing upon the great Universal supply of *Prana*, then using what is given you, allowing the force to pass on to assume some other form. It is the property of all, and all you can do is to use what you need, and allow it to pass on. There is but one Force or Energy, and that is to be found everywhere at all times.

And even the great principle, Mind-substance, is under the same law. It is hard for us to realize this. We are so apt to think of our mental operations as distinctively our own—something that belongs to us personally—that it is difficult for us to realize that Mind-substance is a Universal principle just as Matter or Energy, and that we are but drawing upon the Universal supply in our mental operations. And more than this, the particular portion of Mind-substance that we are using, although separated from the Mind-substance used by other individuals by a thin wall of the very finest kind of Matter, is really in touch with the other apparently separated minds, and with the Universal Mind of which it forms a part. Just as is the Matter of which our physical bodies are composed really in touch with all Matter; and just as is the Vital Force used by us really in touch with all Energy; so is our Mind-substance really in touch with all Mind-substance. It is as if the Ego in its progress were moving through great oceans of Matter, Energy, or Mind-substance, making use of that of each which it needed and which immediately surrounded it, and leaving each behind as it moved on through the great volume of the ocean. This illustration is clumsy, but it may bring to your consciousness a realization that the Ego is the only thing that is really *Yours*, unchangeable and unaltered, and that all the rest is merely that portion of the Universal supply that you draw to yourself for the wants of the moment. It may also bring more clearly before your mind the great Unity of things—may enable you to see things as a Whole, rather than as separated parts. Remember, *You*—the "I"—are the only Real thing about and around you—all that has permanence—and Matter, Force and even Mind-substance, are but your instruments for use and expression. There are great oceans of each surrounding the "I" as it moves along.

It is well for you also to bear in mind the Universality of Life. All of the Universe is alive, vibrating and pulsating with life and energy and motion. There is nothing dead in the Universe. Life is everywhere, and always accompanied by intelligence. There is no such thing as a dead, unintelligent Universe. *Instead of being atoms of Life floating in a sea of death, we are atoms of Life surrounded by an ocean of Life, pulsating, moving, thinking, living.* Every atom of what we call Matter is alive. It has energy or force with it, and is always accompanied by intelligence and life. Look around us as we will—at the animal world—at the plant world—yes, even at the world of minerals and we see life, life, life—all alive and having intelligence. When we are able to bring this conception into the realm of actual consciousness—when we are able not only to intellectually accept this fact, but to even go still further and *feel* and be conscious of this Universal Life on all sides, then are we well on the road to attaining the Cosmic Consciousness.

But all these things are but steps leading up to the realization of the Oneness in Spirit, on the part of the Individual. Gradually there dawns upon him the realization that there is a Unity in the manifestation of Spirit from the Absolute—a unity with itself, and a Union with the Absolute. All this manifestation of Spirit on the part of the Absolute—all this begetting of Divine Children—was in the nature of a single act rather than as a series of acts, if we may be permitted to speak of the manifestation as an *act*. Each Ego is a Centre of Consciousness in this great ocean of Spirit—each is a Real Self, apparently separate from the others and from its source, but the separation is only apparent in both cases, for there is the closest bond of union between the Egos of the Universe of Universes—each is knit to the other in the closest bond of union, and each is still attached to the Absolute by spiritual filaments, if we may use the term. In time we shall grow more conscious of this mutual relationship, as the sheaths are outgrown and cast aside, and in the end we will be withdrawn into the Absolute—shall return to the Mansion of the Father.

It is of the highest importance to the developing soul to unfold into a realization of this relationship and unity, *for when this conception is once fully established the soul is enabled to rise above certain of the lower planes, and is free from the operation of certain laws that bind the undeveloped soul.* Therefore the Yogi teachers are constantly leading the Candidates toward this goal. First by this path, and then by that one, giving them different glimpses of the desired point, until finally the student finds a path best fitted for his feet, and he moves along straight to the mark, and throwing aside the confining bonds that have proved so irksome, he cries aloud for joy at his newfound Freedom.

The following exercises and Mental Drills are intended to aid the Candidate in his work of growing into a realization of his relationship with the Whole of Life and Being.

MENTAL DRILL

(1) Read over what we have said in the *Advanced Course* regarding the principle known as Matter. Realize that all Matter is One at the last—that the real underlying substance of Matter is *Akasa* or Ether, and that all the varying forms evident to our senses are but modifications and grosser forms of that underlying principle. Realize that by known chemical processes all forms of Matter known to us, or rather all combinations resulting in "forms," may be resolved into their original elements, and that these elements are merely *Akasa* in different states of vibration. Let the idea of the Oneness of the visible Universe sink deeply into your mind, until it becomes fixed there. The erroneous conception of diversity in the material world must be replaced by the consciousness of Unity—Oneness, at the last, in spite of the appearance of variety and manifold forms. You must grow to see behind the world of forms of Matter, and see the great principle of Matter (*Akasa* or Ether) back of, within, and under it all. You must grow to *feel* this, as well as to intellectually see it.

(2) Meditate over the last-mentioned truths, and then follow the matter still further. Read what we have said in the *Advanced Course* (Lesson XI) about the last analysis of Matter showing it fading away into Force or Energy until the dividing line is lost, and Matter merges into Energy or Force, showing them both to be but the same thing, Matter being a grosser form of Energy or Force. This idea should be impressed upon the understanding, in order that the complete edifice of the Knowing of the Oneness may be complete in all of its parts.

(3) Then read in the *Advanced Course* about Energy or Force, in the oneness underlying its various manifestations.

79

Consider how one form of Energy may be transformed into another, and so on around the circle, the one principle producing the entire chain of appearances. Realize that the energy within you by which you move and act, is but one of the forms of this great Principle of Energy with which the Universe is filled, and that you may draw to you the required Energy from the great Universal supply. But above all endeavor to grasp the idea of the Oneness pervading the world of Energy or Force, or Motion. See it in its entirety, rather than in its apparent separateness. These steps may appear somewhat tedious and useless, but take our word for it, they are all helps in fitting the mind to grasp the idea of the Oneness of All. Each step is important, and renders the next higher one more easily attained. In this mental drill, it will be well to mentally picture the Universe in perpetual motion—everything is in motion—all matter is moving and changing its forms, and manifesting the Energy within it. Suns and worlds rush through space, their particles constantly changing and moving. Chemical composition and decomposition is constant and unceasing, everywhere the work of building up and breaking down is going on. New combinations of atoms and worlds are constantly being formed and dissolved. And after considering this Oneness of the principle of Energy, reflect that through all these changes of form the Ego—the Real Self—YOU—stand unchanged and unharmed—Eternal, Invincible, Indestructible, Invulnerable, *Real* and Constant among this changing world of forms and force. You are above it all, and it revolves around and about you—Spirit.

(4) Read what we have said in the *Advanced Course* about Force or Energy, shading into Mind-substance which is its parent. Realize that Mind is back of all this great exhi-

bition of Energy and Force that you have been considering. Then will you be ready to consider the Oneness of Mind.

(5) Read what we have said in the *Advanced Course* about Mind-substance. Realize that there is a great world of Mind-substance, or a Universal Mind, which is at the disposal of the Ego. All Thought is the product of the Ego's use of this Mind-substance, its tool and instrument. Realize that this Ocean of Mind is entire and Whole, and that the Ego may draw freely from it. Realize that *You* have this great ocean of Mind at your command, when you unfold sufficiently to use it. Realize that Mind is back of and underneath all of the world of form and names and action, and that in that sense: "All is Mind," although still higher in the scale than even Mind are *You*, the Real Self, the Ego, the Manifestation of the Absolute.

(6) Realize your identity with and relationship to All of Life. Look around you at Life in all its forms, from the lowest to the highest, all being exhibitions of the great principle of Life in operation along different stages of The Path. Scorn not the humblest forms, but look behind the form and see the reality—Life. Feel yourself a part of the great Universal Life. Let your thought sink to the depths of the ocean, and realize your kinship with the Life back of the forms dwelling there. Do not confound the forms (often hideous from your personal point of view) with the principle behind them. Look at the plant life, and the animal life, and seek to see behind the veil of form into the real Life behind and underneath the form. Learn to feel your Life throbbing and thrilling with the Life Principle in these other forms, and in the forms of those of your own race. Gaze into the starry skies and see there the numerous suns and worlds, all peopled with life in some of its myriad forms, and feel your kinship to it. If you can

grasp this thought and consciousness, you will find yourself at-one-ment with those whirling worlds, and, instead of feeling small and insignificant by comparison, you will be conscious of an expansion of Self, until you feel that in those circling worlds is a part of yourself—that You are there also, while standing upon the Earth—that you are akin to all parts of the Universe—nay, more, that they are as much your home as is the spot upon which you are standing. You will find sweeping upon you a sense of consciousness that the Universe is your home—not merely a part of it, as you had previously thought. You will experience a sense of greatness, and broadness and grandness such as you have never dreamed of. You will begin to realize at least a part of your Divine inheritance, and to know indeed that you are a Child of the Infinite, the very essence of your Divine Parent being in the fibres of your being. At such times of realization one becomes conscious of what lies before the soul in its upward path, and how small the greatest prizes that Earth has to offer are when compared to some of these things before the soul, as seen by the eyes of the Spiritual Mind in moments of clear vision.

You must not dispute with these visions of the greatness of the soul, but must treat them hospitably, for they are your very own, coming to you from the regions of your Spiritual Mind which are unfolding into consciousness.

(7) The highest step in this dawning consciousness of the Oneness of All, is the one in which is realized that there is but One Reality, and at the same time the sense of consciousness that the "I" is in that Reality. It is most difficult to express this thought in words for it is something that must be felt, rather than seen by the Intellect. When the Soul realizes that the Spirit within it is, at the last, the only *real* part of it, and that the Absolute and its manifestation as Spirit is

the only *real* thing in the Universe, a great step has been taken. But there is still one higher step to be taken before the full sense of the Oneness and Reality comes to us. That step is the one in which we realize the Identity of the "I" with the great "I" of the Universe. The mystery of the manifestation of the Absolute in the form of the Spirit, is veiled from us—the mind confesses its inability to penetrate behind the veil shielding the Absolute from view, although it will give us a report of its being conscious of the presence of the Absolute just at the edge of the boundary line. But the highest region of the Spiritual Mind, when explored by the advanced souls who are well along the Path, reports that it sees beyond the apparent separation of Spirit from Spirit, and realizes that there is but one Reality of Spirit, and that all the "I's" are really but different views of that One—Centres of Consciousness upon the surface of the One Great "I," the Centre of which is the Absolute Itself. This certainly penetrates the whole region of the Spiritual Mind, and gives us all the message of Oneness of the Spirit, just as the Intellect satisfies us with its message of the Oneness of Matter, Energy, and Mind. The idea of Oneness permeates all planes of Life.

The sense of Reality of the "I" that is apparent to You in the moments of your clearest mental vision, is really the reflection of the sense of Reality underlying the Whole—it is the consciousness of the Whole, manifesting through your point or Centre of Consciousness. The advanced student or Initiate finds his consciousness gradually enlarging until it realizes its identity with the Whole. He realizes that under all the forms and names of the visible world, there is to be found One Life—One Force—One Substance—One Existence—One Reality—ONE. And, instead of his experiencing any sense of the loss of identity or individuality, he becomes conscious of an enlargement of an expansion of individuality or identity—instead of feeling himself absorbed in the Whole, he feels that he is spreading out and embracing the Whole. This is most hard to express in words, for there are no words to fit the conception, and all that we can hope to do is to start into motion, by means of our words, the vibrations that will find a response in the minds of those who read the words, to the end that they will experience the consciousness which will bring its own understanding. This consciousness cannot be transmitted by words proceeding from the Intellect, but vibrations may be set up that will prepare the mind to receive the message from its own higher planes.

Even in the early stages of this dawning consciousness, one is enabled to identify the *real* part of himself with the *real* part of all the other forms of life that pass before his notice. In every other man—in every animal—in every plant—in every mineral—he sees behind the sheath and form of appearance, an evidence of the presence of the Spirit which is akin to his own Spirit—yea, more than akin, for the two are One. He sees Himself in all forms of life, in all time in all places. He realizes that the Real Self is everywhere present and everlasting, and that the Life within himself is also within all the Universe—in everything, for there is nothing dead in the Universe, and all Life, in all of its varying phases, is simply the One Life, held, used and enjoyed in common by all. Each Ego is a Centre of Consciousness in this great ocean of Life, and while apparently separate and distinct, is yet really in touch with the Whole, and with every apparent part.

It is not our intention, in this lesson, to go into the details of this great mystery of Life, or to recite the comparatively little of the Truth that the most advanced teachers and Masters have handed down. This is not the place for it—

it belongs to the subject of Gnani Yoga rather than to Raja Yoga—and we touch upon it here, not for the purpose of trying to explain the scientific side of it to you, but merely in order that your minds may be led to take up the idea and gradually manifest it in conscious realization. There is quite a difference between the scientific, intellectual teaching of Gnani Yoga, whereby the metaphysical and scientific sides of the Yogi teachings are presented to the minds of the students, in a logical, scientific manner, and the methods of Raja Yoga, in which the Candidate is led by degrees to a *consciousness* (outside of mere intellectual belief) of his real nature and powers. We are following the latter plan, for this course is a Course in Raja Yoga. We are aiming to present the matter to the mind in such a manner that it may prepare the way for the dawning consciousness, by brushing away the preconceived notions and prejudices, and allowing a clean entrance for the new conception. Much that we have said in this lesson may appear, on the one hand, like useless repetition, and, on the other hand, like an incomplete presentation of the scientific side of the Yogi teachings. But it will be found, in time, that the effect has been that the mind of the student has undergone a change from the absorbing of the idea of the Oneness of Life, and the Expansion of the Self. The Candidate is urged not to be in too much of a hurry. Development must not be forced. Read what we have written, and practice the Mental Drills we have given, even if they may appear trifling and childish to some of you—we know what they will do for you, and you will agree with us in time. Make haste slowly. You will find that the mind will work out the matter, even though you be engaged in your ordinary work, and have forgotten the subject for the time. The greater portion of mental work is done in this way, while you are busy with something else, or even asleep, for the subconscious portion of the mind works along the lines pointed out for it, and performs its task.

As we have said, the purpose of this lesson is to bring you in the way of the unfoldment of consciousness, rather than to teach you the details of the scientific side of the Yogi teachings. Development is the keynote of Raja Yoga. And the reason that we wish to develop this sense of the Reality of the "I," and the Expansion of the Self, at this place is that thereby you may assert your Mastery over Matter, Energy and Mind. Before you may mount your throne as King, you must fully realize in consciousness that you *are* the *Reality* in this world of appearances. You must realize that you—the *real* You—are not only existent, and real, but that you are in touch with all else that is real, and that the roots of your being are grounded in the Absolute itself. You must realize that instead of being a separate atom of Reality, isolated and fixed in a narrow space, you are a Centre of Consciousness in the Whole of Reality, and that the Universe of Universes is your home—that your Centre of Consciousness might be moved on to a point trillions of miles from the Earth (which distance would be as nothing in Space) and still you—the awakened soul—would be just as much at home there as here—that even while you are here, your influence extends far out into space. Your real state, which will be revealed to you, gradually, throughout the ages, is so great and grand, that your mind in its present state of development cannot grasp even the faint reflection of that glory.

We wish you to try to form at least a faint idea of your Real State of Being, in order that you may control the lower principles by the force of your awakened Will, which Will depends upon your degree of consciousness of the Real Self.

As man grows in understanding and consciousness of the Real Self, so does his ability to use his Will grow. Will is the attribute of the Real Self. It is well that this great realization of the Real Self brings with it Love for all of Life, and Kindness, for, were it not so, the Will that comes to him who grows into a realization of his real being could be used to the great hurt of those of the race who had not progressed so far (their *relative* hurt, we mean, for in the end, and at the last, no soul is ever really *hurt*). But the dawning power brings with it greater Love and Kindness, and the higher the soul mounts the more is it filled with the higher ideals and the more does it throw from it the lower animal attributes. It is true that some souls growing into a consciousness of their real nature, without an understanding of what it all means, may commit the error of using the awakened Will for self-ish ends, as may be seen in the cases of the Black Magicians spoken of in the occult writings, and also in the cases of well-known characters in history and in modern life, who manifest an enormous Will which they misuse. All of this class of people of great Will have stumbled or grown blindly into a consciousness (or partial consciousness) of the real nature, but lack the restraining influence of the higher teachings. But such misuse of the Will brings pain and unrest to the user, and he is eventually driven into the right road.

We do not expect our students to grasp fully this idea of the Expansion of Self. Even the highest grasp it only partially. But until you get a glimmering of the consciousness you will not be able to progress far on the path of Raja Yoga. You must understand *what you are*, before you are able to use the power that lies dormant within you. You must realize that you are the Master, before you can claim the powers of the Master, and expect to have your commands obeyed. So bear patiently with us, your Teachers, while we set before you the lessons to be learned—the tasks to be performed. The road is long, and is rough in places—the feet may become tired and bruised, but the reward is great, and there are resting places along the path. Be not discouraged if your progress seem slow, for the soul must unfold naturally as does the flower, without haste, without force.

And be not dismayed nor affrighted if you occasionally catch a glimpse of your higher self. As "M.C."[3] says, in her notes on *Light on the Path* (see *Advanced Course*):

> To have seen thy soul in its bloom, is to have obtained a momentary glimpse in thyself of the transfiguration which shall eventually make thee more than man; to recognize, is to achieve the great task of gazing upon the blazing light without dropping the eyes, and not falling back in terror as though before some ghastly phantom. This happens to some, and so, when the victory is all but won, it is lost.

Peace be with thee.

There is but one ultimate form of Matter; one ultimate form of Energy; one ultimate form of Mind. Matter proceeds from Energy, and Energy from Mind, and all are an emanation of the Absolute, threefold in appearance but One in substance. There is but One Life, and that permeates the Universe, manifesting in various forms, but being, at the last, but One. My body is one with Universal Matter; My energy and vital force is one with the Universal Energy; My Mind is one with the Universal Mind; My Life is one with the Universal Life. The Absolute has expressed and manifested itself in Spirit, which is the real "I" overshadowing and embracing all the apparently separate "I's." "I" feel my identity with Spirit and realize the Oneness of All Reality. I feel my unity with all Spirit, and my Union (through Spirit) with the Absolute. I realize that "I" am an Expression and Manifestation of the Absolute, and that its very essence is within me. I am filled with Divine Love. I am filled with Divine Power. I am filled with Divine Wisdom. I am conscious of identity in spirit, in substance; and in nature; with the One Reality.

Mental Control

In our first three lessons of this series, we have endeavored to bring into realization within your mind (1) the consciousness of the "I"; its independence from the body; its immortality; its invincibility and invulnerability; (2) the superiority of the "I" over the mind, as well as over the body; the fact that the mind is not the "I," but is merely an instrument for the expression of the "I"; the fact that the "I" is master of the mind, as well as of the body; that the "I" is behind all thought; that the "I" can set aside for consideration the sensations, emotions, passions, desires, and the rest of the mental phenomena, and still realize that it, the "I," is apart from these mental manifestations, and remains unchanged, real and fully existent; that the "I" can set aside any and all of its mental tools and instruments, as "not I" things, and still consciously realize that after so setting them aside there remains something—itself—the "I" which cannot be set aside or taken from; that the "I" is the master of the mind, and not its slave; (3) that the "I" is a much greater thing than the little personal "I" we have been considering it to be; that the "I" is a part of that great One Reality which pervades all the Universe; that it is connected with all other forms of life by countless ties, mental and spiritual filaments and relations; that the "I" is a Centre of Consciousness in that great One Reality or Spirit, which is behind and back of all Life and Existence, the Centre of which Reality or Existence, is the Absolute or God; that the sense of Reality that is inherent in the "I," is really the reflection of the sense of Reality inherent in the Whole—the Great "I" of the Universe.

The underlying principle of these three lessons is the Reality of the "I," in itself, over and above all Matter, Force, or Mind—positive to all of them, just as they are positive or negative to each other—and negative only to the Centre of the One—the Absolute itself. And this is the position for the Candidate or Initiate to take:

> I am positive to Mind, Energy, and Matter, and control them all—I am negative only to the Absolute, which is the Centre of Being, of which Being I Am. And, as I assert my mastery over Mind, Energy, and Matter, and exercise my Will over them, so do I acknowledge my subordination to the Absolute, and gladly open my soul to the inflow of the Divine Will, and partake of its Power, Strength, and Wisdom.

In the present lesson, and those immediately following it, we shall endeavor to assist the Candidate or Initiate in acquiring a mastery of the subordinate manifestations, Matter, Energy, and Mind. In order to acquire and assert this mastery, one must acquaint himself with the nature of the thing to be controlled.

In our *Advanced Course* we have endeavored to explain

to you the nature of the Three Great Manifestations, known as *Chitta*, or Mind-Substance; *Prana*, or Energy; and *Akasa*, or the Principle of Matter. We also explained to you that the "I" of man is superior to these three, being what is known as *Atman* or Spirit. Matter, Energy, and Mind, as we have explained, are manifestations of the Absolute, and are relative things. The Yogi philosophy teaches that Matter is the grossest form of manifested substance, being below Energy and Mind, and consequently negative to, and subordinate to both. One stage higher than Matter, is Energy or Force, which is positive to, and has authority over, Matter (Matter being a still grosser form of substance), but which is negative to and subordinate to Mind, which is a still higher form of substance. Next in order comes the highest of the three—Mind—the finest form of substance, and which dominates both Energy and Matter, being positive to both. Mind, however, is negative and subordinate to the "I," which is Spirit, and obeys the orders of the latter when firmly and intelligently given. The "I" itself is subordinate only to the Absolute—the Centre of Being—the "I" being positive and dominant over the threefold manifestation of Mind, Energy, and Matter.

The "I," which for the sake of the illustration must be regarded as a separate thing (although it is really only a Centre of Consciousness in the great body of Spirit), finds itself surrounded by the triple-ocean of Mind, Energy and Matter, which ocean extends into Infinity. The body is but a physical form through which flows an unending stream of matter, for, as you know the particles and atoms of the body are constantly changing; being renewed; replaced; thrown off, and supplanted. One's body of a few years ago, or rather the particles composing that body, have passed off and now form new combinations in the world of matter. And one's body of today is passing away and being replaced by new particles. And one's body of next year is now occupying some other portion of space, and its particles are now parts of countless other combinations, from which space and combinations they will later come to combine and form the body of next year. There is nothing permanent about the body—even the particles of the bones are being constantly replaced by others. And so it is with the Vital Energy, Force, or Strength of the body (including that of the brain). It is constantly being used up, and expended, a fresh supply taking its place. And even the Mind of the person is changeable, and the Mind-substance or *Chitta*, is being used up and replenished, the new supply coming from the great Ocean of Mind, into which the discarded portion slips, just as is the case with the matter and energy.

While the majority of our students, who are more or less familiar with the current material scientific conceptions, will readily accept the above idea of the ocean of Matter, and Energy, and the fact that there is a continual using up and replenishing of one's store of both, they may have more or less trouble in accepting the idea that Mind is a substance or principle amenable to the same general laws as are the other two manifestations, or attributes of substance. One is so apt to think of his Mind as "himself"—the "I." Notwithstanding the fact that in our Second Lesson of this series we showed you that the "I" is superior to the mental states, and that it can set them aside and regard and consider them as "not-I" things, yet the force of the habit of thought is very strong, and it may take some of you considerable time before you "get into the way" of realizing that your Mind is "something that you use," instead of being You—yourself. And yet, you must

94

persevere in attaining this realization, for in the degree that you realize your dominance over your mind, so will be your control of it, and its amenability to that control. And, as is the degree of that dominance and control, so will be the character, grade and extent of the work that your Mind will do for you. So you see: *Realization brings Control—and Control brings results.* This statement lies at the base of the science of Raja Yoga. And many of its first exercises are designed to acquaint the student with that realization, and to develop the realization and control by habit and practice.

The Yogi Philosophy teaches that instead of Mind being the "I," it is the thing through and by means of which the "I" *thinks*, at least so far as is concerned the knowledge concerning the phenomenal or outward Universe—that is the Universe of Name and Form. There is a higher Knowledge locked up in the innermost part of the "I," that far transcends any information that it may receive about or from the outer world, but that is not before us for consideration at this time, and we must concern ourselves with the "thinking" about the world of things.

Mind-substance in Sanskrit is called *Chitta*, and a wave in the *Chitta* (which wave is the combination of Mind and Energy) is called *Vritta*, which is akin to what we call a "thought." In other words it is "mind in action," whereas *Chitta* is "mind in repose." *Vritta*, when literally translated means "a whirlpool or eddy in the mind," which is exactly what a thought really is.

But we must call the attention of the student, at this point, to the fact that the word "Mind" is used in two ways by the Yogis and other occultists, and the student is directed to form a clear conception of each meaning, in order to avoid confusion, and that he may more clearly perceive the two aspects of the things which the word is intended to express. In the first place the word "Mind" is used as synonymous with *Chitta*, or Mind-substance, which is the Universal Mind Principle. From this *Chitta*, Mind-substance, or Mind, all the material of the millions of personal minds is obtained. The second meaning of the word "Mind" is that which we mean when we speak of the "mind" of anyone, thereby meaning the mental faculties of that particular person—that which distinguishes his mental personality from that of another. We have taught you that this "mind" in Man, functions on three planes, and have called the respective manifestations (1) the Instinctive Mind; (2) the Intellect; and (3) the Spiritual Mind. (See *Fourteen Lessons in Yogi Philosophy*, etc.) These three mental planes, taken together, make up the "mind" of the person, or to be more exact they, clustered around the "I," form the "soul" of the individual. The word "soul" is often used as synonymous with "spirit" but those who have followed us will distinguish the difference. The "soul" is the Ego surrounded by its mental principles, while the Spirit is the "soul of the soul"—the "I," or Real Self.

The Science of Raja Yoga, to which this series of lessons is devoted, teaches, as its basic principle, the Control of the Mind. It holds that the first step toward Power consists in obtaining a control of one's own mind. It holds that the internal world must be conquered before the outer world is attacked. It holds that the "I" manifests itself in Will, and that that Will may be used to manipulate, guide, govern and direct the mind of its owner, as well as the physical world. It aims to clear away all mental rubbish, and encumbrances— to conduct a "mental house-cleaning," as it were, and to secure a clear, clean, healthy mind. Then it proceeds to control that mind intelligently, and with effect, saving all waste-power, and by means of concentration bringing the Mind in full harmony with the Will, that it may be brought to a focus and its power greatly increased and its efficiency fully secured. Concentration and Willpower are the means by which the Yogis obtain such wonderful results, and by which they manage and direct their vigorous, healthy minds, and master the material world, acting positively upon Energy and Matter. This control extends to all planes of the Mind and the Yogis not only control the Instinctive Mind, holding in subjection its lower qualities and making use of its other parts, but they also develop and enlarge the field of their Intellect and obtain from it wonderful results. Even the Spiritual Mind is mastered, and aided in its unfoldment, and urged to pass down into the field of consciousness some of the wonderful secrets to be found within its area. By means of Raja Yoga many of the secrets of existence and Being—many of the Riddles of the Universe—are answered and solved. And by it the latent powers inherent in the constitution of Man are unfolded and brought into action. Those highly advanced in the science are believed to have obtained such a wonderful degree of power and control over the forces of the universe, that they are as gods compared with the ordinary man.

Raja Yoga teaches that not only may power of this kind be secured, but that a wonderful field of Knowledge is opened out through its practice. It holds that when the concentrated mind is focused upon thing or subject, the true nature and inner meaning, of, and concerning, that thing or subject will be brought to view. The concentrated mind passes through the object or subject just as the X-ray passes through a block of wood, and the thing is seen by the "I" as it *is*—in truth—and not as it had appeared before, imperfectly and erroneously. Not only may the outside world be thus explored, but the mental ray may be turned inward, and the secret places of the mind explored. When it is remembered that the bit of mind that each man possesses, is like a drop of the ocean which contains within its tiny compass all the elements that make up the ocean, and that to know perfectly the drop is to know perfectly the ocean, then we begin to see what such a power really means.

Many in the Western world who have attained great results in the intellectual and scientific fields of endeavor, have developed these powers more or less unconsciously. Many great inventors are practical Yogis, although they do not realize the source of their power. Anyone who is familiar with the personal mental characteristics of Edison, will see that he follows some of the Raja Yoga methods, and that Concentration is one of his strongest weapons. And from all reports, Prof. Elmer Gates, of Washington, DC, whose mind has unfolded many wonderful discoveries and inventions, is also a practical Yogi although he may repudiate the assertion vigorously, and may not have familiarized himself with the principles of this science, which he has "dropped into" unconsciously. Those who have reported upon Prof. Gates's methods, say that he fairly "digs out" the inventions and discoveries from his mind, after going into seclusion and practicing concentration, and what is known as the Mental Vision.

But we have given you enough of theory for one lesson, and must begin to give you directions whereby you may aid yourself in developing these latent powers and unfolding these dormant energies. You will notice that in this series we first tell you something about the theory, and then proceed to give you "something to do." This is the true Yogi method as followed and practiced by their best teachers. Too much theory is tiresome, and sings the mind to sleep, while too much exercise tires one, and does not give the inquiring part of his mind the necessary food. To combine both in suitable proportions is the better plan, and one that we aim to follow.

MENTAL DRILL AND EXERCISES

Before we can get the mind to do good work for us, we must first "tame" it, and bring it to obedience to the Will of the "I." The mind, as a rule, has been allowed to run wild, and follow its own sweet will and desires, without regard to anything else. Like a spoiled child or badly trained domestic animal, it gets into much trouble, and is of very little pleasure, comfort or use. The minds of many of us are like menageries of wild animals, each pursuing the bent of its own nature, and going its own way. We have the whole menagerie within us— the tiger, the ape, the peacock, the ass, the goose, the sheep the hyena, and all the rest. And we have been letting these animals rule us. Even our Intellect is erratic, unstable, and like the quicksilver to which the ancient occultists compared it, shifting and uncertain. If you will look around you you will see that those men and women in the world who have really accomplished anything worthwhile have trained their minds to obedience. They have asserted the Will over their own minds, and learned Mastery and Power in that way. The average mind chafes at the restraint of the Will, and is like a frisky monkey that will not be "taught tricks." But taught it must be, if it wants to do good work. And teach it you must if you expect to get any use from it—if you expect to use it, instead of having it use you.

And this is the first thing to be learned in Raja Yoga— this control of the mind. Those who had hoped for some royal road to mastery, may be disappointed, but there is only one way and that is to master and control the mind by the Will. Otherwise it will run away when you most need it. And so we shall give you some exercise designed to aid you in this direction.

The first exercise in Raja Yoga is what is called *Pratyahara* or the art of making the mind introspective or turned inward upon itself. It is the first step toward mental control. It aims to turn the mind from going outward, and gradually turning it inward upon itself or inner nature. The object is to gain control of it by the Will. The following exercises will aid in that direction:

Exercise I

(a) Place yourself in a comfortable position, and so far as possible free from outside disturbing influences. Make no violent effort to control the mind, but rather allow it to run along for a while and exhaust its efforts. It will take advantage of the opportunity, and will jump around like an unchained monkey at first, until it gradually slows down and looks to you for orders. It may take some time to tame down at first trial, but each time you try it will come around to you in shorter time. The Yogis spend much time in acquiring this mental peace and calm, and consider themselves well paid for it.

(b) When the mind is well calmed down, and peaceful, fix the thought on the "I Am," as taught in our previous lessons. Picture the "I" as an entity independent of the body; deathless; invulnerable; immortal; real. Then think of it as independent of the body, and able to exist without its fleshly covering. Meditate upon this for a time, and then gradually direct the thought to the realization of the "I" as independent and superior to the mind, and controlling same. Go over the general ideas of the first two lessons, and endeavor to calmly reflect upon them and to see them in the "mind's eye." You will find that your mind is gradually becoming more and more peaceful and calm, and that the distracting thoughts of the outside world are farther and farther removed from you.

(c) Then let the mind pass on to a calm consideration of the Third Lesson, in which we have spoken of the Oneness of All, and the relationship of the "I" to the One Life; Power; Intelligence; Being. You will find that you are acquiring a mental control and calm heretofore unknown to you. The exercises in the first three lessons will have prepared you for this.

(d) The following is the most difficult of the variations or degrees of this exercise, but the ability to perform it will come gradually. The exercise consists in gradually shutting out all thought or impression of the outside world; of the body; and of the thoughts themselves, the student concentrating and meditating upon the word and idea "I AM," the idea being that he shall concentrate upon the idea of mere "being" or "existence," symbolized by the words "I Am." Not "I am *this*," or "I am *that*," or "I *do* this," or "I *think* that," but simply: "I *AM*." This exercise will focus the attention at the very centre of Being within oneself, and will gather in all the mental energies, instead of allowing them to be scattered upon outside things. A feeling of Peace, Strength, and Power will result, for the affirmation, and the thought back of it, is the most powerful and strongest that one may make, for it is a statement of Actual Being, and a turning of the thought inward to that truth. Let the mind first dwell upon the word "I," identifying it with the Self, and then let it pass on to the word

"AM," which signifies Reality, and Being. Then combine the two with the meanings thereof, and the result a most powerful focusing of thought inward, and most potent Statement of Being.

It is well to accompany the above exercises with a comfortable and easy physical attitude, so as to prevent the distraction of the attention by the body. In order to do this one should assume an easy attitude and then relax every muscle, and take the tension from every nerve, until a perfect sense of ease, comfort and relaxation is obtained. You should practice this until you have fully acquired it. It will be useful to you in many ways, besides rendering Concentration and Meditation easier. It will act as a "rest cure" for tired body, nerves, and mind.

Exercise II

The second step in Raja Yoga is what is known as *Dharana*, or Concentration. This is a most wonderful idea in the direction of focusing the mental forces, and may be cultivated to an almost incredible degree, but all this requires work, time, and patience. But the student will be well repaid for it. Concentration consists in the mind focusing upon a certain subject, or object, and being held there for a time. This, at first thought seems very easy, but a little practice will show how difficult it is to firmly fix the attention and hold it there. It will have a tendency to waver, and move to some other object or subject, and much practice will be needed in order to hold it at the desired point. But practice will accomplish wonders, as one may see by observing people who have acquired this faculty, and who use it in their everyday life.

But the following point should be remembered. Many persons have acquired the faculty of concentrating their attention, but have allowed it to become almost involuntary, and they become a slave to it, forgetting themselves and everything else, and often neglecting necessary affairs. This is the ignorant way of concentrating, and those addicted to it become slaves to their habits, instead of masters of their minds. They become daydreamers, and absentminded people, instead of Masters. They are to be pitied as much as those who cannot concentrate at all. The secret is in a mastery of the mind. The Yogis can concentrate at will, and completely bury themselves in the subject before them, and extract from it every item of interest, and can then pass the mind from the thing at will, the same control being used in both cases. They do not allow fits of abstraction, or "absentmindedness" to come upon them, nor are they daydreamers. On the contrary they are very wide-awake individuals; close observers; clear thinkers; correct reasoners. They are masters of their minds, not slaves to their moods. The ignorant concentrator buries himself in the object or subject, and allows it to master and absorb himself, while the trained Yogi thinker asserts the "I," and then directs his mind to concentrate upon the subject or object, keeping it well under control and in view all the time. Do you see the difference? Then heed the lesson.

The following exercises may be found useful in the first steps of Concentration:

(a) Concentrate the attention upon some familiar object—a pencil, for instance. Hold the mind there and consider the pencil to the exclusion of any other object. Consider its size; color; shape; kind of wood. Consider its uses, and purposes; its materials; the process of its manufacture, etc.,

etc., etc. In short think as many things about the pencil as possible allowing the mind to pursue any associated bypaths, such as a consideration of the graphite of which the "lead" is made; the forest from which came the wood used in making the pencil; the history of pencils, and other implements used for writing, etc. In short exhaust the subject of "Pencils." In considering a subject under concentration, the following plan of synopsis will be found useful. Think of the thing in question from the following viewpoints:

(1) The thing itself.
(2) The place from whence it came.
(3) Its purpose or use.
(4) Its associations.
(5) Its probable end.

Do not let the apparently trivial nature of the inquiry discourage you, for the simplest form of mental training is useful, and will help to develop your Will and Concentration. It is akin to the process of developing a physical muscle by some simple exercise, and in both cases one loses sight of the unimportance of the exercise itself, in view of the end to be gained.

(b) Concentrate the attention upon some part of the body—the hand for instance, and fixing your entire attention upon it, shut off or inhibit all sensation from the other parts of the body. A little practice will enable you to do this. In addition to the mental training, this exercise will stimulate the part of the body concentrated upon, for reasons that will appear in future lessons. Change the parts of the body concentrated upon, and thus give the mind a variety of exercises, and the body the effect of a general stimulation.

(c) These exercises may be extended indefinitely upon familiar objects about you. Remember always, that the thing in itself is of no importance, the whole idea being to train the mind to obey the Will, so that when you really wish to use the mental forces upon some important object, you may find them well trained and obedient. Do not be tempted to slight this part of the work because it is "dry" and uninteresting, for it leads up to things that are most interesting, and opens a door to a fascinating subject.

(d) Practice focusing the attention upon some abstract subject—that is upon some subject of interest that may offer a field for mental exploration. Think about the subject in all its phases and branches, following up one bypath, and then another, until you feel that you know all about the subject that your mind has acquired. You will be surprised to find how much more you know about any one thing or subject than you had believed possible. In hidden corners of your mind you will find some useful or interesting information about the thing in question, and when you are through you will feel well posted upon it, and upon the things connected with it. This exercise will not only help, to develop your intellectual powers, but will strengthen your memory, and broaden your mind, and give you more confidence in yourself. And, in addition, you will have taken a valuable exercise in Concentration or *Dharana*.

The Importance of Concentration

Concentration is a focusing of the mind. And this focusing of the mind requires a focusing, or bringing to a center, of the Will. The mind is concentrated because the Will is focused upon the object. The mind flows into the mould made by the Will. The above exercises are designed not only to accustom the mind to the obedience and direction of the Will, but also tend to accustom the Will to command. We speak of strengthening the Will, when what we really mean is training the mind to obey, and accustoming the Will to command. Our Will is strong enough, but we do not realize it. The Will takes root in the very center of our being—in the "I," but our imperfectly developed mind does not recognize this tact. We are like young elephants that do not recognize their own strength, but allow themselves to be mastered by puny drivers, whom they could brush aside with a movement. The Will is back of all action—all doing—mental and physical.

We shall have much to say touching the Will, in these lessons, and the student should give the matter his careful attention. Let him look around him, and he will see that the great difference between the men who have stepped forward from the ranks, and those who remain huddled up in the crowd, consists in Determination and Will. As Buxton has well said: "The longer I live, the more certain I am that the great difference between men, the feeble and the powerful; the great and the insignificant; is Energy and Invincible Determination." And he might have added that the thing behind that "energy and invincible determination" was Will.

The writers and thinkers of all ages have recognized the wonderful and transcendent importance of the Will. Tennyson sings: "O living Will thou shalt endure when all that seems shall suffer shock." Oliver Wendell Holmes says:

> The seat of the Will seems to vary with the organ through which it is manifested; to transport itself to different parts

of the brain, as we may wish to recall a picture, a phrase, a melody; to throw its force on the muscles or the intellectual processes. Like the general-in-chief, its place is everywhere in the field of action. It is the least like an instrument of any of our faculties; the furthest removed from our conceptions of mechanism and matter, as we commonly define them.

Holmes was correct in his idea, but faulty in his details. The Will does not change its seat, which is always in the center of the Ego, but the Will forces the mind to all parts, and in all directions, and it directs the *Prana* or vital force likewise. The Will is indeed the general-in-chief, but it does not rush to the various points of action, but sends its messengers and couriers there to carry out its orders. Buxton has said: "The Will will do anything that can be done in this world. And no talents, no circumstances, no opportunities will make a two-legged creature a Man without it." Ik Marvel truly says:

> Resolve is what makes a man manifest; not puny resolve, not crude determinations, not errant purpose—but that strong and indefatigable Will which treads down difficulties and danger, as a boy treads down the heaving frost-lands of winter; which kindles his eye and brain with a proud pulse-beat toward the unattainable. Will makes men giants.

The great obstacle to the proper use of the Will, in the case of the majority of people, is the lack of ability to focus the attention. The Yogis clearly understand this point, and many of the Raja Yoga exercises which are given to the students by the teachers, are designed to overcome this difficulty. Attention is the outward evidence of the Will. As a French writer has said: "The attention is subject to the superior authority of the Ego. I yield it, or I withhold it, as I please. I direct it in turn to several points. I concentrate it upon each point as long as my Will can stand the effort." Prof. James has said: "The essential achievement of the Will, when it is most voluntary, is to attend to a difficult object, and hold it fast before the mind. Effort of Attention is the essential phenomenon of the Will." And Prof. Halleck says: "The first step toward the development of Will lies in the exercise of Attention. Ideas grow in distinctness and motor-power as we attend to them. If we take two ideas of the same intensity and center the attention upon one, we shall notice how much it grows in power." Prof. Sully says: "Attention may be roughly defined as the active self-direction of the mind to any object which presents itself at the moment." The word "Attention" is derived from two Latin words, *ad tendere*, meaning "to stretch towards," and this is just what the Yogis know it to be. By means of their psychic or clairvoyant sight, they see the thought of the attentive person stretched out toward the object attended to, like a sharp wedge, the point of which is focused upon the object under consideration, the entire force of the thought being concentrated at that point. This is true not only when the person is considering an object, but when he is earnestly impressing his ideas upon another, or upon some task to be accomplished. Attention means reaching the mind out to and focusing it upon something.

The trained Will exhibits itself in a tenacious Attention, and this Attention is one of the signs of the trained Will. The student must not hastily conclude that this kind of Attention is a common faculty among men. On the contrary it is quite rare, and is seen only among those of "strong" mentality. Anyone may fasten his Attention upon some passing, *pleasing* thing, but it takes a trained will to fasten it upon some unattractive thing, and hold it there. Of course the trained occultist is able to throw interest into the most unattractive thing upon which it becomes advisable to focus his Attention, but this, in itself, comes with the trained Will, and is not the possession of the average man. Voluntary Attention is rare, and is found only among strong characters. But it may be cultivated and grown, until he who has scarcely a shade of it today, in time may become a giant. It is all a matter of practice, exercise, and Will.

It is difficult to say too much in favor of the development of the faculty of tenacious Attention. One possessing this developed faculty is able to accomplish far more than even a much "brighter" man who lacks it. And the best way to train the Attention, under the direction of the Will, is to practice upon *uninteresting* objects, and ideas, holding them before the mind until they begin to assume an Interest. This is difficult at first, but the task soon begins to take on a pleasant aspect, for one finds that his Willpower and Attention are growing, and he feels himself acquiring a Force and Power that were lacking before—he realizes that he is growing Stronger. Charles Dickens said that the secret of his success consisted in his developing a faculty of throwing his entire Attention into whatever he happened to be doing at the moment and then being able to turn that same degree of Attention to the next thing coming before him for consideration. He was like a man behind a great searchlight, which was successively turned upon point after point, illuminating each in turn. The "I" is the man behind the light, and the Will is the reflector, the light being the Attention.

This discussion of Will and Attention may seem somewhat "dry" to the student, but that is all the more reason that he should attend to it. It is the secret that lies at the basis of the Science of Raja Yoga, and the Yogi Masters have attained a degree of Concentrated Will and Attention that would be inconceivable to the average "man on the street." By reason of this, they are able to direct the mind here and there, outward or inward, with an enormous force. They are able to focus the mind upon a small thing with remarkable intensity, just as the rays of the sun may be focused through a "sunglass" and caused to ignite linen, or, on the other hand, they are able to send forth the mind with intense energy, illuminating whatever it rests upon, just as happens in the case of the strong electric searchlight, with which many of us are familiar. By all means start in to cultivate the Attention and Will. Practice on the unpleasant tasks—do the things that you have before you, and from which you have been shrinking because they were unpleasant. Throw interest into them, and the difficulty will vanish, and you will come out of it much stronger, and filled with a new sense of Power.

FOURTH LESSON—MANTRAM

"I" have a Will—it is my inalienable property
and right. I determine to cultivate and develop
it by practice and exercise. My mind is
obedient to my Will. I assert my Will over my
Mind. I am Master of my mind and body.
I *assert* my Mastery. My Will is Dynamic—full
of Force and Energy, and Power.
I feel my strength. I am Strong. I am Forceful.
I am Vital. I am Center of Consciousness,
Energy, Strength, and Power, and I claim
my birthright.

Cultivation of Attention

In our last lesson we called your attention to the fact that the Yogis devote considerable time and practice to the acquirement of Concentration. And we also had something to say regarding the relation of Attention to the subject of Concentration. In this lesson we shall have more to say on the subject of Attention, for it is one of the important things relating to the practice of Raja Yoga, and the Yogis insist upon their students practicing systematically to develop and cultivate the faculty. Attention lies at the base of Willpower, and the cultivation of one makes easy the exercise of the other.

To explain why we lay so much importance to the cultivation of Attention, would necessitate our anticipating future lessons of this series, which we do not deem advisable at this time. And so we must ask our students to take our word for it, that all that we have to say regarding the importance of the cultivation of Attention, is occasioned by the relation of that subject to the use of the mind in certain directions as will appear fully later on.

In order to let you know that we are not advancing some peculiar theory of the Yogis, which may not be in harmony with modern Western Science, we give you in this article a number of quotations, from Western writers and thinkers, touching upon this important faculty of the mind, so that you may see that the West and East agree upon this main point, however different may be their explanations of the fact, or their use of the power gained by the cultivation of Attention.

As we said in our last lesson, the word Attention is derived from two Latin words "*ad tendere*," meaning "to stretch toward," which is really what Attention is. The "I" wills that the mind be focused on some particular object or thing, and the mind obeys and "stretches toward" that object or thing, focusing its entire energy upon it, observing every detail, dissecting, analyzing, consciously and subconsciously, drawing to itself every possible bit of information regarding it, both from within and from without. We cannot lay too much stress upon the acquirement of this great faculty, or rather, the development of it, for it is necessary for the intelligent study of Raja Yoga.

In order to bring out the importance of the subject, suppose we start in by actually giving our Attention to the subject of Attention, and see how much more there is in it than we had thought. We shall be well repaid for the amount of time and trouble expended upon it.

Attention has been defined as a focusing of consciousness, or, if one prefers the form of expression, as "detention in consciousness." In the first case, we may liken it to the action of the sunglass through which the sun's rays are concentrated upon an object, the result being that the heat is gathered together at a small given point, the intensity of the same being raised many degrees until the heat is sufficient to burn a piece of wood, or evaporate water. If the rays were not focused, the same rays and heat would have been scattered over a large surface, and the effect and power lessened. And so it is with the mind. If it is allowed to scatter itself over the entire field of a subject, it will exert but little power and the results will be weak. But if it is passed through the sunglass of attention, and focused first over one part, and then over another, and so on, the matter may be mastered in detail, and a result accomplished that will seem little less than marvelous to those who do not know the secret.

Thompson has said: "The experiences most permanently impressed upon consciousness, are those upon which the greatest amount of attention has been fixed."

Another writer upon the subject has said that "Attention is so essentially necessary to understanding, that without some degree of it the ideas and perceptions that pass through the mind seem to leave no trace behind them."

Hamilton has said: "An act of attention, that is, an act of concentration, seems thus necessary to every exertion of consciousness, as a certain contraction of the pupil is requisite to every exertion of vision. Attention then is to consciousness what the contraction of the pupil is to sight, or, to the eye of the mind what the microscope or telescope is to the bodily eye. It constitutes the better half of all intellectual power."

And Brodie adds, quite forcibly: "It is Attention much more than any difference in the abstract power of reasoning, which constitutes the vast difference which exists between minds of different individuals."

Butler gives us this important testimony: "The most important intellectual habit I know of is the habit of attending exclusively to the matter in hand. It is commonly said that genius cannot be infused by education, yet this power of concentrated attention, which belongs as a part of his gift to every great discoverer, is unquestionably capable of almost indefinite augmentation by resolute practice."

And, concluding this review of opinions, and endorsements of that which the Yogis have so much to say, and to which they attach so much importance, let us listen to the words of Beattie, who says: "The force wherewith anything strikes the mind, is generally in proportion to the degree of attention bestowed upon it. Moreover, the great art of memory is attention, and inattentive people always have bad memories."

There are two general kinds of Attention. The first is the Attention directed within the mind upon mental objects and concepts. The other is the Attention directed outward upon objects external to ourselves. The same general rules and laws apply to both equally.

Likewise there may be drawn another distinction and division of attention into two classes, *viz.*, Attention attracted by some impression coming into consciousness without any conscious effort of the Will—this is called Involuntary Attention, for the Attention and Interest is caught by the attractiveness or novelty of the object. Attention directed to some object by an effort of the Will, is called Voluntary Attention. Involuntary Attention is quite common, and requires no special training. In fact, the lower animals, and young children seem to have a greater share of it than do adult men. A great percentage of men and women never get beyond this stage to any marked degree. On the other hand, Voluntary Attention requires effort, will, and determination—a certain mental training, that is beyond the majority of people, for they will not "take the trouble" to direct their attention in this way. Voluntary Attention is the mark of the student and other thoughtful men. They focus their minds on objects that do not yield immediate interest or pleasure, in order that they may learn and accomplish. The careless person will not thus fasten his Attention, at least not more than a moment or so, for his Involuntary Attention is soon attracted by some passing object of no matter how trifling a nature, and the Voluntary Attention disappears and is forgotten. Voluntary Attention is developed by practice and perseverance, and is well worth the trouble, for nothing in the mental world is accomplished without its use.

The Attention does not readily fasten itself to uninteresting objects, and, unless interest can be created it requires a considerable degree of Voluntary Attention in order that the mind may be fastened upon such an object. And, more than this, even if the ordinary attention is attracted it will soon waver, unless there is some interesting change in the aspect of the object, that will give the attention a fresh hold of interest, or unless some new quality, characteristic or property manifests itself in the object. This fact occurs because the mind mechanism has not been trained to bear prolonged Voluntary Attention, and, in fact, the physical brain is not accustomed to the task, although it may be so trained by patient practice.

It has been noticed by investigators that the Attention may be rested and freshened, either by withdrawing the Voluntary Attention from the object, and allowing the Attention to manifest along Involuntary lines toward passing objects, etc.; or, on the other hand, by directing the Voluntary Attention into a new field of observation—toward some new object. Sometimes one plan will seem to give the best results, and again the other will seem preferable.

We have called your attention to the fact that Interest develops Attention, and holds it fixed, while an uninteresting object or subject requires a much greater effort and application. This fact is apparent to anyone. A common illustration may be found in the matter of reading a book. Nearly everyone will give his undivided attention to some bright, thrilling story, while but few are able to use sufficient Voluntary Attention to master the pages of some scientific work. But, right here, we wish to call your attention to the other side of the case, which is another example of the fact that Truth is composed of paradoxes.

Just as Interest develops Attention, so it is a truth that Attention develops Interest. If one will take the trouble to give a little Voluntary Attention to an object, he will soon find that a little perseverance will bring to light points of Interest in the object. Things before unseen and unsuspected, are quickly brought to light. And many new phases, and aspects of the subject or object are seen, each one of which, in turn, becomes an object of Interest. This is a fact not so generally known, and one that it will be well for you to remember, and to use in practice. *Look* for the interesting features of an uninteresting thing, and they will appear to your view, and before long the uninteresting object will have changed into a thing having many-sided interests.

Voluntary Attention is one of the signs of a developed Will. That is, of a mind that has been well trained by the Will, for the Will is always strong, and it is the mind that has to be trained, not the Will. And on the other hand, one of the best ways to train the mind by the Will, is by practice in Voluntary Attention. So you see how the rule works both ways. Some Western psychologists have even advanced theories that the Voluntary Attention is the *only* power of the Will,

and that that power is sufficient, for if the Attention be firmly fixed, and held upon an object the mind will "do the rest."
We do not agree with this school of philosophers, but merely
mention the fact as an illustration of the importance attributed by psychologists to this matter of Voluntary Attention.

A man of a strongly developed Attention often accomplishes far more than some much brighter man who lacks it.
Voluntary Attention and Application is a very good substi-
tute for Genius, and often accomplishes far more in the long
run.

Voluntary Attention is the fixing of the mind earnestly
and intently upon some particular object, at the same time
shutting out from consciousness other objects pressing for
entrance. Hamilton has defined it as "consciousness voluntarily applied under its law of limitations to some determi-
nate object." The same writer goes on to state that "the greater
the number of objects to which our consciousness is simul-
taneously extended, the smaller is the intensity with which it
is able to consider each, and consequently the less vivid and
distinct will be the information it contains of the several objects. When our interest in any particular object is excited,
and when we wish to obtain all the knowledge concerning
it in our power, it behooves us to limit our consideration to
that object to the exclusion of others."

The human mind has the power of attending to only one
object at a time, although it is able to pass from one object
to another with a marvelous degree of speed, so rapidly, in
fact, that some have held that it could grasp several things
at once. But the best authorities, Eastern and Western, hold
to the "single idea" theory as being correct. On this point we
may quote a few authorities.

Jouffroy says that "It is established by experience that

we cannot give our attention to two different objects at the same time." And Holland states that "Two thoughts, however closely related to one another, cannot be presumed to exist at the same time." And Lewes has told us that "The nature of our organism prevents our having more than one aspect of an object at each instant presented to consciousness." Whateley says: "The best philosophers are agreed that the mind cannot actually attend to more than one thing at a time, but, when it appears to be doing so it is really shifting with prodigious rapidity backward and forward from one to the other."

By giving a concentrated Voluntary Attention to an object, we not only are able to see and think about it with the greatest possible degree of clearness, but the mind has a tendency, under such circumstances, to bring into the field of consciousness all the different ideas associated in our memory with that object or subject, and to build around the object or subject a mass of associated facts and information. And at the same time the Attention given the subject makes more vivid and clear all that we learn about the thing at the time, and, in fact, all that we may afterwards learn about it. It seems to cut a channel, through which knowledge flows.

Attention magnifies and increases the powers of perception, and greatly aids the exercise of the perceptive faculties. By "paying attention" to something seen or heard, one is enabled to observe the details of the thing seen or heard, and where the inattentive mind acquires say three impressions the attentive mind absorbs three times three, or perhaps three times "three times three," or twenty-seven. And, as we have just said, Attention brings into play the powers of association, and gives us the "loose end" of an almost infinite chain of associated facts, stored away in our memory, forming new combinations of facts which we had never grouped

together before, and bring out into the field of consciousness all the many scraps of information regarding the thing
to which we are giving attention. The proof of this is within the experience of everyone. Where is the one who does
not remember sitting down to some writing, painting, reading, etc., with interest and attention, and finding, much to his
surprise, what a flow of facts regarding the matter in hand
was passing through his mind. Attention seems to focus all
the knowledge of a thing that you possess, and by bringing
it to a point enables you to combine, associate, classify, etc.,
and thus create new knowledge. Gibbon tells us that after he
gave a brief glance and consideration to a new subject, he
suspended further work upon it, and allowed his mind (under concentrated attention) to bring forth all his associated
knowledge regarding the subject, after which he renewed the
task with increased power and efficiency.

The more one's attention is fixed upon a subject under
consideration, the deeper is the impression which the subject
leaves upon the mind. And the easier will it be for him to afterwards pursue the same train of thought and work.

Attention is a prerequisite of good memory, and in fact
there can be no memory at all unless some degree of attention is given. The degree of memory depends upon the degree of attention and interest. And when it is considered that
the work of today is made efficient by the memory of things
learned yesterday, the day before yesterday, and so on, it is
seen that the degree of attention given today regulates the
quality of the work of tomorrow.

Some authorities have described Genius as the result
of great powers of attention, or, at least, that the two seem
to run together. Some writer has said that "possibly the best
definition of genius is the power of concentrating upon some

one given subject until its possibilities are exhausted and absorbed." Simpson has said that "The power and habit of thinking closely and continuously upon the subject at hand, to the exclusion, for the time, of all other subjects, is one of the principal, if, indeed, not the principal, means of success." Sir Isaac Newton has told us his plan of absorbing information and knowledge. He has stated that he would keep the subject under consideration before him continually, and then would wait till the first dawning of perception gradually brightened into a clear light, little by little. A mental sunrise, in fact.

That sage observer Dr. Abercrombie has written that he considered that he knew of no more important rule for rising to eminence in any profession or occupation than the ability to do one thing at a time, avoiding all distracting and diverting objects or subjects, and keeping the leading matter continually before the mind. And others have added that such a course will enable one to observe relations between the subject and other things that will not be apparent to the careless observer or student.

The degree of Attention cultivated by a man is the degree of his capacity for intellectual work. As we have said, the "great" men of all walks of life have developed this faculty to a wonderful degree, and many of them seem to get results "intuitively," whereas, in truth, they obtain them by reason of their concentrated power of Attention, which enables them to see right into the center of a subject or proposition—and all around it, back and front, and all sides, in a space of time incredible to the man who has not cultivated this mighty power. Men who have devoted much attention to some special line of work or research, are able to act almost as if they possessed "second sight," providing the subject is within their favorite field of endeavor. Attention quickens every one of the faculties—the reasoning faculties—the senses—the deriding qualities—the analytical faculties, and so on, each being given a "fine edge" by their use under a concentrated Attention.

And, on the other hand, there is no surer indication of a weak mind than the deficiency in Attention. This weakness may arise from illness or physical weakness reacting upon the brain, in which case the trouble is but temporary. Or it may arise from a lack of mental development. Imbeciles and idiots have little or no Attention. The great French psychologist Luys, speaking of this fact, says:

> Imbeciles and idiots see badly, hear badly, feel badly, and their sensorium is, in consequence, in a similar condition of sensitive poverty. Its impressionability for the things of the external world is at a minimum, its sensibility weak, and consequently, it is difficult to provoke the physiological condition necessary for the absorption of the external impression.

In old age the Attention is the first faculty to show signs of decay. Some authorities have held that the Memory was the first faculty to be affected by the approach of old age, but this is incorrect, for it is a matter of common experience that the aged manifest a wonderfully clear memory of events occurring in the far past. The reason that their memory of recent events is so poor is because their failing powers of Attention has prevented them from receiving strong, clear mental impressions, and as is the impression so is the memory. Their early impressions having been clear and strong, are easily recalled, while their later ones, being weak, are recalled with difficulty. If the Memory were at fault, it would be difficult for them to recall any impression, recent or far distant in time.

But we must stop quoting examples and authorities, and urging upon you the importance of the faculty of Attention. If you do not now realize it, it is because you have not given the subject the Attention that you should have exercised, and further repetition would not remedy matters.

Admitting the importance of Attention, from the psychological point of view, not to speak of the occult side of the subject, is it not a matter of importance for you to start in to cultivate that faculty? We think so. And the only way to cultivate any mental or physical part or faculty is to Exercise it. Exercise "uses up" a muscle, or mental faculty, but the organism makes haste to rush to the scene additional material—cell-stuff, nerve force, etc., to repair the waste, and it always sends a little more than is needed. And this "little more," continually accruing and increasing, is what increases the muscles and brain centers. And improved and strengthened brain centers give the mind better instruments with which to work.

One of the first things to do in the cultivation of Attention is to learn to think of, and do, one thing at a time. Acquiring the "knack" or habit of attending closely to the things before us, and then passing on to the next and treating it in the same way, is most conducive to success, and its practice is the best exercise for the cultivation of the faculty of Attention. And on the contrary, there is nothing more harmful from the point of view of successful performance—and nothing that will do more to destroy the power of giving Attention—than the habit of trying to do one thing while thinking of another. The thinking part of the mind, and the acting part should work together, not in opposition.

Dr. Beattie, speaking of this subject, tells us "It is a mat-

ter of no small importance that we acquire the habit of doing only one thing at a time; by which I mean that while attending to any one object, our thoughts ought not to wander
to another." And Granville adds, "A frequent cause of failure
in the faculty of Attention is striving to think of more than
one thing at a time." And Kay quotes, approvingly, a writer who says: "She did things easily, because she attended to
them in the doing. When she made bread, she thought of the
bread, and not of the fashion of her next dress, or of her partner at the last dance." Lord Chesterfield said, "There is time
enough for everything in the course of the day, if you do but
one thing at a time; but there is not time enough in the year if
you try to do two things at a time."

To attain the best results one should practice concentrating upon the task before him, shutting out, so far as possible,
every other idea or thought. One should even forget self—
personality—in such cases, as there is nothing more destruc-
tive of good thinking than to allow morbid self-consciousness to intrude. One does best when he "forgets himself" in
his work, and sinks his personality in the creative work. The
"earnest" man or woman is the one who sinks personality in
the desired result, or performance of the task undertaken.
The actor, or preacher, or orator, or writer, must lose sight
of himself to get the best results. Keep the Attention fixed on
the thing before you, and let the self take care of itself.

In connection with the above, we may relate an anecdote of Whateley that may be interesting in connection with
the consideration of this subject of "losing one's self" in the
task. He was asked for a recipe for "bashfulness," and replied
that the person was bashful simply because he was thinking of himself and the impression he was making. His recipe
was that the young man should think of others—of the plea-

sure he could give them—and in that way he would forget all about himself. The prescription is said to have effected the cure. The same authority has written, "Let both the extempo-rary speaker, and the reader of his own compositions, study to avoid as far as possible all thoughts of self, earnestly fix-ing the mind on the matter of what is delivered; and they will feel less that embarrassment which arises from the thought of what opinion the hearers will form of them."

The same writer, Whateley, seems to have made quite a study of Attention and has given us some interesting infor-mation on its details. The following may be read with inter-est, and if properly understood may be employed to advan-tage. He says, "It is a fact, and a very curious one, that many people find that they can best attend to any serious matter when they are occupied with something else which requires a little, and but a little, attention, such as working with the needle, cutting open paper leaves, or, for want of some such employment, fiddling anyhow with the fingers." He does not give the reason for this, and at first sight it might seem like a contradiction of the "one thing at a time" idea. But a clos-er examination will show us that the minor work (the cutting leaves, etc.) is in the nature of an involuntary or automatic movement, inasmuch as it requires little or no voluntary at-tention, and seems to "do itself." It does not take off the At-tention from the main subject, but perhaps acts to catch the "waste Attention" that often tries to divide the Attention from some voluntary act to another. The habit mind may be doing one thing, while the Attention is fixed on another. For instance, one may be writing with his attention firmly fixed upon the thought he wishes to express, while at the time his hand is doing the writing, apparently with no attention being given it. But, let a boy, or person unaccustomed to writing, try to express his thoughts in this way, and you will find that he is hampered in the flow of his thoughts by the fact that he has to give much attention to the mechanical act of writing. In the same way, the beginner on the typewriter finds it difficult to compose to the machine, while the experienced typist finds the mechanical movements no hindrance whatever to the flow of thought and focusing of Attention; in fact, many find that they can compose much better while using the typewriter than they can by dictating to a stenographer. We think you will see the principle.

And now for a little Mental Drill in Attention, that you may be started on the road to cultivate this important faculty.

MENTAL DRILL IN ATTENTION

Exercise I

Begin by taking some familiar object and placing it before you, try to get as many impressions regarding it as is possible for you. Study its shape, its color, its size, and the thousand and one little peculiarities about it that present themselves to your attention. In doing this, reduce the thing to its simplest parts—analyze it as far as is possible—dissect it, mentally, and study its parts in detail. The more simple and small the part to be considered, the more clearly will the impression be received, and the more vividly will it be recalled. Reduce the thing to the smallest possible proportions, and then examine each portion, and mastering that, then pass on to the next part, and so on, until you have covered the entire field. Then, when you have exhausted the object, take a pencil and paper and put down as nearly as possible all the things or details of the object examined. When you have done this, compare the written description with the object itself, and see how many things you have failed to note.

The next day take up the same object, and after reexamining it, write down the details and you will find that you will have stored away a greater number of impressions regarding it, and, moreover, you will have discovered many new details during your second examination. This exercise strengthens the memory as well as the Attention, for the two are closely connected, the memory depending largely upon the clearness and strength of the impressions received, while the impressions depend upon the amount of attention given to the thing observed. Do not tire yourself with this exercise, for a tired Attention is a poor Attention. Better try it by degrees, increasing the task a little each time you try it. Make a game of it if you like, and you will find it quite interesting to notice the steady but gradual improvement.

It will be interesting to practice this in connection with some friend, varying the exercise by both examining the object, and writing down their impressions, separately, and then comparing results. This adds interest to the task, and you will be surprised to see how rapidly both of you increase in your powers of observation, which powers, of course, result from Attention.

Exercise II

This exercise is but a variation of the first one. It consists in entering a room, and taking a hasty glance around, and then walking out, and afterward writing down the number of things that you have observed, with a description of each. You will be surprised to observe how many things you have missed at first sight, and how you will improve in observation by a little practice. This exercise, also, may be improved by the assistance of a friend, as related in our last exercise. It is astonishing how many details one may observe and remember, after a little practice. It is related of Houdin, the French conjurer, that he improved and developed his faculty of Attention and Memory by playing this game with a young relative. They would pass by a shop window, taking a hasty, attentive glance at its contents. Then they would go around the corner and compare notes. At first they could remember only a few prominent articles—that is, their Attention could grasp only a few. But as they developed by practice, they found that they could observe and remember a vast number of things and objects in the window. And, at last, it is related that Houdin could pass rapidly before any large shop window, bestowing upon it but one hasty glance, and then tell the names of, and closely describe, nearly every object in plain sight in the window. The feat was accomplished by the fact that the cultivated Attention enabled Houdin to fasten upon his mind a vivid mental image of the window and its contents, and then he was able to describe the articles one by one from the picture in his mind.

Houdin taught his son to develop Attention by a simple exercise which may be interesting and of value to you. He would lay down a domino before the boy—a five-four, for example. He would require the boy to tell him the combined number at once, without allowing him to stop to count the spots, one by one. "Nine" the boy would answer after a moment's hesitation. Then another domino, a three-four, would be added. "That makes sixteen," cried the boy. Two dominoes at a time was the second day's task. The next day, three was the standard. The next day, four, and so on, until the boy was able to handle twelve dominoes—that is to say, give instantaneously the total number of spots on twelve dominoes, after a single glance. This was Attention, in earnest, and shows what practice will do to develop a faculty. The result was shown by the wonderful powers of observation, memory and attention, together with instantaneous mental action, that the boy developed. Not only was he able to add dominoes instantaneously, but he had powers of observation, etc., that seemed little short of miraculous. And yet it is related that he had poor attention, and deficient memory to begin with.

If this seems incredible, let us remember how old whist players note and remember every card in the pack, and can tell whether they have been played or not, and all the circumstances attending upon them. The same is true of chess players, who observe every move and can relate the whole game in detail long after it has been played. And remember, also, how one woman may pass another woman on the street, and without seeming to give her more than a careless glance, may be able to relate in detail every feature of the other woman's apparel, including its color, texture, style of fashioning, probable price of the material, etc., etc. And a mere man would have noticed scarcely anything about it—because he would not have given it any attention. But how soon would that man learn to equal his sister in attention and observation of women's wearing apparel, if his business success depended upon it, or if his speculative instinct was called into play by a wager with some friend as to who could remember the most about a woman's clothing, seen in a passing glance? You see it is all a matter of Interest and Attention.

But we forget that the Attention may be developed and cultivated, and we complain that we "cannot remember things," or that we do not seem to be able to "take notice." A little practice will do wonders in this direction.

Now, while the above exercises will develop your memory and powers of observation, still that is not the main reason that we have given them to you. We have an ulterior object, that will appear in time. We aim to develop your Willpower, and we know that Attention stands at the gate of Willpower. In order to be able to use your Will, you must be able to focus the Attention forcibly and distinctly. And these childish exercises will help you to develop the mental muscles of the Attention. If you could but realize the childish games the young Yogi students are required to play, in order to develop the mental faculties, you would change your minds about the Yogi Adepts whom you have been thinking about as mere dreamers, far removed from the practical. These men, and their students, are intensely practical. They have gained the mastery of the Mind, and its faculties, and are able to use them as sharp-edged tools, while the untrained man finds that he has but a dull, unsharpened blade that will do nothing but hack and hew roughly, instead of being able to produce the finished product. The Yogi believes in giving the "I" good tools with which to work, and he spends much time in tempering and sharpening these tools. Oh, no, the Yogi are not idle dreamers. Their grasp of "practical things" would surprise many a practical, matter-of-fact Western businessman, if he could but observe it.

And so, we ask you to practice "observing things." The two exercises we have given are but indications of the general line. We could give you thousands, but you can prepare them yourselves as well as could we. The little Hindu boy is taught Attention by being asked to note and remember the number, color, character and other details of a number of colored stones, jewelry, etc., shown for an instant in an open palm, the hand being closed the moment after. He is taught to note and describe passing travelers, and their equipages—houses he sees on his journeys—and thousands of other everyday objects. The results are almost marvelous. In this way he is prepared as a *chela* or student, and he brings to his *guru* or teacher a brain well developed—a mind thoroughly trained to obey the Will of the "I"—and with faculties quickened to perceive instantly that which others would fail to see in a fortnight. It is true that he does not turn these faculties to "business" or other so-called "practical" pursuits, but prefers to devote them to abstract studies and pursuits outside of that which the Western man considers to be the end and aim of life. But remember that the two civilizations are quite different—following different ideals—having different economic conditions—living in different worlds, as it were. But that is all a matter of taste and ideals—the faculty for the "practical life" of the West is possessed by the *chela*, if he saw fit to use it. But all Hindu youths are not *chelas*, remember—nor are all Western youths "captains of industry," or Edisons.

FIFTH LESSON—MANTRAMS

I am using my Attention to develop
my mental faculties, so as to give the "I"
a perfect instrument with which to work.
The mind is *My* instrument and I am bringing it
to a state of capacity for perfect work.

There is but One Life—One Life Underlying.
This Life is manifesting through ME, and through
every other shape, form, and thing. I am resting
on the bosom of the Great Ocean of Life,
and it is supporting me, and will carry me safely,
though the waves rise and fall—though the storms
rage and the tempests roar. I am safe on the
Ocean of Life, and rejoice as I feel the sway of its
motion. Nothing can harm me—though changes
may come and go, I am Safe. I am One with the
All Life, and its Power, Knowledge, and Peace are
behind, underneath, and within Me. O! One Life!
express Thyself through me—carry me now on the
crest of the wave, now deep down in the trough of
the ocean—supported always by Thee—all is good
to me, as I feel Thy life moving in and through
me. I am Alive, through thy life, and I open
myself to thy full manifestation and inflow.

Cultivation of Perception

Man gains his knowledge of the outside world through his senses. And, consequently, many of us are in the habit of thinking of these senses as if *they* did the sensing, instead of being merely carriers of the vibrations coming from the outside world, which are then presented to the Mind for examination. We shall speak of this at greater length a little later on in this lesson. Just now we wish to impress upon you the fact that it is the Mind that perceives, not the senses. And, consequently, a development of Perception is really a development of the Mind.

The Yogis put their students through a very arduous course of practice and exercises designed to develop their powers of perception. To many this would appear to be merely a development of the Senses, which might appear odd in view of the fact that the Yogis are constantly preaching the folly of being governed and ruled by the senses. But there is nothing paradoxical about all this, for the Yogis, while preaching the folly of sense life, and manifesting the teaching in their lives, nevertheless believe in any and all exercises calculated to "sharpen" the Mind, and develop it to a keen state and condition.

They see a great difference between having a sharpened perception, on the one hand, and being a slave to the senses on the other. For instance, what would be thought of a man who objected to acquiring a keen eyesight, for fear it would lead him away from higher things, by reason of his becoming attached to the beautiful things he might see. To realize the folly of this idea, one may look at its logical conclusion, which would be that one would then be much better off if all their senses were destroyed. The absurdity, not to say wickedness, of such an idea will be apparent to everyone, after a minute's consideration.

The secret of the Yogi theory and teachings regarding the development of the Mental powers, lies in the word "*Mastery.*" The Yoga student accomplishes and attains this mastery in two ways. The first way is by subordinating all the feelings, sense-impressions, etc., to the Mastery of the "I," or Will, the Mastery being obtained in this way by the assertion of the dominancy of the "I" over the faculties and emotions, etc. The second step, or way, lies in the Yogi, once having asserted the mastery, beginning to develop and perfect the Mental instrument, so as to get better work and returns from it. In this way he increases his kingdom and is Master over a much larger territory.

In order for one to gain knowledge, it is necessary to use to the best advantage the mental instruments and tools that he finds at his disposal. And again, one must develop and improve such tools—put a keen edge upon them, etc. Not only does one gain a great benefit from a development of the faculties of perception, but he also acquires an additional benefit from the training of the whole mind arising from the mental discipline and training resulting from the former exercises, etc. In our previous lessons we have pointed out some of the means by which these faculties might be greatly improved, and their efficiency increased. In this lesson we shall point out certain directions in which the Perceptive faculties may be trained. We trust that the simplicity of the idea may not cause any of our students to lose interest in the work. If they only knew just what such development would lead to they would gladly follow our suggestions in the matter. Every one of the ideas and exercises given by us are intended to lead up to the strengthening of the Mind, and the attainment of powers and the unfoldment of faculties. There is no royal road to Raja Yoga, but the student will be well repaid for the work of climbing the hill of Attainment.

In view of the above, let us examine the question of The Senses. Through the doors of the senses Man receives all his information regarding the outside world. If he keeps these doors but half open, or crowded up with obstacles and rubbish, he may expect to receive but few messages from outside. But if he keeps his doorways clear, and clean, he will obtain the best that is passing his way.

If one were born without sense-organs—no matter how good a Mind he might have—he would be compelled to live his life in a dreamy plant-life stage of existence, with little or no consciousness. The Mind would be like a seed in the earth, that for some reason was prevented from growing.

One may object that the highest ideas do not come to us through the senses, but the reply is that the things obtained through the senses are the "raw material" upon which the mind works, and fashions the beautiful things that it is able to produce in its highest stages. Just as is the body dependent for growth upon the nourishment taken into it, so is the mind dependent for growth upon the impressions received from the Universe—and these impressions come largely through the senses. It may be objected to that we know many things that we have not received through our senses. But, does the objector include the impressions that came through his senses in some previous existence, and which have been impressed upon his instinctive mind, or soul-memory? It is true that there are higher senses than those usually recognized, but Nature insists upon one learning the lessons of the lower grades before attempting those of the higher.

Do not forget that all that we know we have "worked for." There is nothing that comes to the idler, or shirker. What we know is merely the result of "stored-up accumulations of previous experience," as Lewes has so well said.

So it will be seen that the Yogi idea that one should develop all parts of the Mind is strictly correct, if one will take the trouble to examine into the matter. A man sees and knows but very little of what is going on about him. His limitations are great. His powers of vision report only a few vibrations of light, while below and above the scale lie an infinity of vibrations unknown to him. The same is true of the powers of hearing, for only a comparatively small portion of the soundwaves reach the Mind of Man—even some of the animals hear more than he does.

If a man had only one sense he would obtain but a one-sense idea of the outside world. If another sense is added his knowledge is doubled. And so on. The best proof of the relation between increased sense perception and development is had in the study of the evolution of animal forms. In the early stages of life the organism has only the sense of feeling—and very dim at that—and a faint sense of taste. Then developed smell, hearing and sight, each marking a distinct advance in the scale of life, for a new world has been opened out to the advancing forms of life. And, when man develops new senses—and this is before the race—he will be a much wiser and greater being.

Carpenter, many years ago, voiced a thought that will be familiar to those who are acquainted with the Yogi teachings regarding the unfoldment of new senses. He said:

It does not seem at all improbable that there are properties of matter of which none of our senses can take immediate cognizance, and which other beings might be formed to perceive in the same manner as we are sensible to light, sound, etc.

And Isaac Taylor said:

It may be that within the field occupied by the visible and ponderable universe there is existing and moving another element fraught with another species of life—corporeal, indeed, and various in its orders, but not open to cognizance of those who are confined to the conditions of animal organization. Is it to be thought that the eye of man is the measure of the Creator's power?—and that He created nothing but that which he has exposed to our present senses? The contrary seems much more than barely possible; ought we not to think it almost certain?

Another writer. Prof. Masson, has said:

If a new sense or two were added to the present normal

139

number, in man, that which is now the phenomenal world for all of us might, for all that we know, burst into something amazingly different and wider, in consequence of the additional revelations of these new senses.

But not only is this true, but Man may increase his powers of knowledge and experience if he will but develop the senses he has to a higher degree of efficiency, instead of allowing them to remain comparatively atrophied. And toward this end, this lesson is written.

The Mind obtains its impressions of objects of the outside world by means of the brain and sense organs. The sensory organs are the instruments of the Mind, as is also the brain and the entire nervous system. By means of the nerves, and the brain, the Mind makes use of the sensory organs in order that it may obtain information regarding external objects.

The senses are usually said to consist of five different forms, *viz.*, sight, hearing, smell, touch, and taste. The Yogis teach that there are higher senses, undeveloped, or comparatively so, in the majority of the race, but toward the unfoldment of which the race is tending. But we shall not touch upon these latent senses in this lesson, as they belong to another phase of the subject. In addition to the five senses above enumerated, some physiologists and psychologists have held that there were several others in evidence. For instance, the sense by which the inner organs revealed their presence and condition. The muscular system reports to the mind through some sense that is not that of "touch," although closely allied to it. And the feelings of hunger, thirst, etc., seem to come to us through an unnamed sense.

Bernstein has distinguished between the five senses and the one just referred to as follows:

The characteristic distinction between these common sensations and the sensations of the senses is that by the latter we gain knowledge of the occurrences and objects which belong to the external world (and which sensations we refer to external objects), whilst by the former we only feel conditions of our own body.

A sensation is the internal, mental conception, resulting from an external object or fact exciting the sense organs and nerves, and the brain, thus making the mind "aware" of the external object or fact. As Bain has said, it is the "mental impression, feeling, or conscious state, resulting from the action of external things on some part of the body, called on that account, sensitive."

Each channel of sense impressions has an organ, or organs, peculiarly adapted for the excitation of its substance by the particular kind of vibrations through which it receives impressions. The eye is most cunningly and carefully designed to receive the light waves; and sound waves produce no effect upon it. And, likewise, the delicate mechanism of the ear responds only to sound waves; light waves failing to register upon it. Each set of sensations is entirely different, and the organs and nerves designed to register each particular set are peculiarly adapted to their own special work. The organs of sense, including their special nervous systems, may be compared to a delicate instrument that the mind has fashioned for itself, that it may investigate, examine and obtain reports from the outside world.

We have become so accustomed to the workings of the senses that we take them as a "matter of course," and fail to recognize them as the delicate and wonderful instruments that they are—designed and perfected by the mind for its own use. If we will think of the soul as designing, manufacturing and using these instruments, we may begin to understand their true relations to our lives, and, accordingly treat them with more respect and consideration.

We are in the habit of thinking that we are aware of all the sensations received by our mind. But this is very far from being correct. The unconscious regions of the mind are incomparably larger than the small conscious area that we generally think of when we say "my mind." In future lessons we shall proceed to consider this wonderful area, and examine what is to be found there. Taine has well said:

> There is going on within us a subterranean process of infinite extent; its products alone are known to us, and are only known to us in the mass. As to elements, and their elements, consciousness does not attain to them. They are to sensations what secondary molecules and primitive molecules are to bodies. We get a glance here and there at obscure and infinite worlds extending beneath our distinct sensations. These are compounds and wholes. For their elements to be perceptible to consciousness, it is necessary for them to be added together, and so to acquire a certain bulk and to occupy a certain time, for if the group does not attain this bulk, and does not last this time, we observe no changes in our state. Nevertheless, though it escapes us, there is one.

But we must postpone our consideration of this more than interesting phase of the subject, until some future lesson, when we shall take a trip into the regions of Mind, under and above Consciousness. And a most wonderful trip many of us will find it, too.

For the present, we must pay our attention to the channels by which the material for knowledge and thought enter our minds. For these sense impressions, coming to us from without, are indeed "material" upon which the mind works in order to manufacture the product called "Thought."

This material we obtain through the channels of the senses, and then store in that wonderful storehouse, the Memory, from whence we bring out material from time to time, which we proceed to weave into the fabric of Thought. The skill of the worker depends upon his training, and his ability to select and combine the proper materials. And the acquiring of good materials to be stored up is an important part of the work.

A mind without stored-up material of impressions and experiences would be like a factory without material. The machinery would have nothing upon which to work, and the shop would be idle. As Helmholtz[4] has said:

Apprehension by the senses supplies directly or indirectly, the material of all human knowledge, or at least the stimulus necessary to develop every inborn faculty of the mind.

And Herbert Spencer,[5] has this to say of this phase of the subject:

It is almost a truism to say that in proportion to the numerousness of the objects that can be distinguished, and in proportion to the variety of coexistences and sequences that can be severally responded to, must be the number and rapidity and variety of the changes within the organism— must be the amount of vitality.

A little reflection upon this subject will show us that

the greater degree of exercise and training given the senses, the greater the degree of mental power and capability. As we store our mental storehouse with the materials to be manu-factured into thought, so is the quality and quantity of the fabric produced.

It therefore behooves us to awaken from our "lazy" con-dition of mind, and to proceed to develop our organs of sense, and their attendant mechanism, as by doing so we in-crease our capacity for thought and knowledge.

Before passing to the exercises, however, it may be well to give a hasty passing glance at the several senses, and their peculiarities.

The sense of Touch is the simplest and primal sense. Long before the lower forms of life had developed the high-er senses, they had evidenced the sense of Touch or Feel-ing. Without this sense they would have been unable to have found their food, or to receive and respond to outside im-pressions. In the early forms of life it was exercised equally by all parts of the body, although in the higher forms this sense has become somewhat localized, as certain parts of the body are far more sensitive than are others. The skin is the seat of the sense of Touch, and its nerves are distribut-ed over the entire area of the skin. The hand, and particular-ly the fingers, and their tips, are the principal organs of this sense.

The acuteness of Touch varies materially in different parts of the body. Experiments have shown that a pair of compasses would register impressions as a very slight dis-tance apart when applied to the tip of the tongue. The dis-tance at which the two points could be distinguished from one point, on the tip of the tongue, was called "one line." Us-ing this "line" as a standard, it was found that the palmar surface of the third finger registered 2 lines; the surface of the lips 4 lines, and the skin of the back, and on the middle of the arm or thigh, as high as 60 lines. The degree of sensitiveness to Touch varies greatly with different individuals, some having a very fine sense of touch in their fingers, while others manifested a very much lower degree.

In the same way, there is a great difference in the response of the fingers to weight—a great difference in the ability to distinguish the difference of the weight of objects. It has been found that some people can distinguish differences in weight down to very small fractions of an ounce. Fine distinctions in the differences in temperature have also been noticed.

The sense of touch and its development has meant much for Man. It is the one sense in which Man surpasses the animals in the matter of degree and acuteness. The animal may have a keener smell, taste, hearing and sight, but its sense of Touch is far beneath that of Man. Anaxagoras is quoted as saying that "if the animals had hands and fingers, they would be like men."

In developing the sense of Touch, the student must remember that Attention is the key to success. The greater the amount of Attention the greater the degree of development possible in the case of any sense. When the Attention is concentrated upon any particular sense, the latter becomes quickened and more acute, and repeated exercise, under the stimulus of Attention, will work wonders in the case of any particular sense. And on the other hand, the sense of touch may be almost, or completely inhibited, by firmly fixing the Attention upon something else. As an extreme proof of this latter fact, the student is asked to remember the fact that men have been known to suffer excruciating torture, apparently without feeling, owing to the mind being intently riveted upon some idea or thought. As Wyld has said:

> The martyr borne above sensuous impressions, is not only able to endure tortures, but is able to endure and quench them. The pinching and cutting of the flesh only added energy to the death song of the American Indian, and even the slave under the lash is sustained by the indignant sense of his wrongs.

In the cases of persons engaged in occupations requiring a fine degree of Touch, the development is marvelous. The engraver passes his hand over the plate, and is able to distinguish the slightest imperfection. And the handler of cloth and fabrics is able to distinguish the finest differences, simply by the sense of touch. Wool sorters also exercise a wonderfully high degree of fineness of touch. And the blind are able to make up for the loss of sight by their greatly increased sense of Touch, cases being recorded where the blind have been able to distinguish *color* by the different "feel" of the material.

The sense of Taste is closely allied to that of Touch—in fact some authorities have considered Taste as a very highly developed sense of Touch in certain surfaces of the body, the tongue notably. It will be remembered that the tongue has the finest sense of Touch, and it also has the sense of Taste developed to perfection. In Taste and Touch the object must be brought in direct contact with the organ of sense, which is not the case in Smell, Hearing, or Sight. And, be it remembered, that the latter senses have special nerves, while Taste is compelled to fall back upon the ordinary nerves of Touch. It is true that Taste is confined to a very small part of the surface of the body, while Touch is general. But this only indicates a special development of the special area. The sense of Taste also depends to a great extent upon the presence of fluids, and only substances that are soluble make their presence known through the organs and sense of Taste.

Physiologists report that the sense of Taste in some persons is so acute that one part of strychnine in one million parts of water has been distinguished. There are certain occupations, such as that of wine-tasters, tea-tasters, etc., the followers of which manifest a degree of fineness of Taste almost incredible.

The sense of Smell is closely connected with the sense of Taste, and often acts in connection therewith, as the tiny particles of the substance in the mouth arise to the organs of Smell, by means of the opening or means of communication situated in the back part of the mouth. Besides which the nose usually detects the odor of substances before they enter the mouth. The sense of Smell operates by reason of the tiny particles or the object being carried to the mucous membrane of the interior of the nose, by means of the air. The membrane, being moist, seizes and holds these particles for a moment, and the fine nervous organism reports differences and qualities and the Mind is thus informed of the nature of the object.

The sense of Smell is very highly developed among animals, who are compelled to rely upon it to a considerable extent. And many occupations among men require the development of this sense, for instance, the tobacconist, the wine dealer, the perfumers, the chemist, etc. It is related that in the cases of certain blind people, it has been observed that they could distinguish persons in this manner.

The sense of Hearing is a more complex one than in the case of Taste, Touch and Smell. In the latter three the objects to be sensed must be brought in close contact with the sense-organs, while in Hearing the object may be far removed, the impressions being carried by the vibrations of the air, which are caught up and reported upon by the nervous organism of the sense of Hearing. The internal mechanism of the ear is most wonderfully intricate and complex, and excites to wonder the person examining it. It cannot be described here for want of space, but the student is advised to inquire into it if he has access to any library containing books on the subject. It is a wonderful illustration of the work of the mind in building up for itself instruments with which to work—to acquire knowledge.

The ear records vibrations in the air from 20 or 32 per second, the rate of the lowest audible note, to those of 38,000 per second, the rate of the highest audible note. There is a great difference in individuals in regard to the fineness of the sense of Hearing. But all may develop this sense by the application of Attention. The animals and savages have wonderfully acute senses of Hearing developed only along the lines of distinctness, however—on the other hand musicians have developed the sense along different lines.

The sense of Sight is generally conceded to be the highest and most complex of all the senses of Man. It deals with a far larger number of objects—at longer distances—and gives a far greater variety of reports to the mind than any of its associate senses. It is the sense of Touch magnified many times. As Wilson says of it:

> Our sight may be considered as a more delicate and diffusive kind of touch that spreads itself over an infinite number of bodies; comprehends the largest figures, and brings into our reach some of the most remote parts of the universe.

The sense of Sight receives its impressions from the outside world by means of waves that travel from body to body—from sun to earth, and from lamp to eye. These waves of light arise from vibrations in substance, of an almost incredible degree of rapidity. The lowest light vibration is about 450,000,000,000,000 per second, while the highest is about 750,000,000,000,000 per second. These figures deal only with the vibrations recognizable by the eye as light. Above and below these figures of the scale are countless other degrees invisible to the eye, although some of them may be recorded by instruments. The different sensations of color, depend upon the rate of the vibrations, red being the limit of the lowest, and violet the limit of the highest visible vibrations—orange, yellow, green, blue, and indigo being the intermediate rates or colors.

The cultivation of the sense of Sight, under the aid of Attention is most important to all persons. By being able to clearly see and distinguish the parts of an object, a degree of knowledge regarding it is obtained that one may not acquire without the said exercise of the faculty. We have spoken of this under the subject of Attention, in a previous lesson, to which lesson we again refer the student. The fixing of the eye upon an object has the power of concentrating the thoughts and preventing them from wandering. The eye has other properties and qualities that will be dwelt upon in future lessons. It has other uses than seeing. The influence of the eye is a marvelous thing, and may be cultivated and developed.

We trust that what we have said will bring the student to a realization of the importance of developing the powers of Perception. The senses have been developed by the mind during a long period of evolution and effort that surely would not have been given unless the object in view was worth it all. The "I" insists upon obtaining knowledge of the Universe, and much of this knowledge may be obtained only through the senses. The Yogi student must be "wide awake" and possessed of developed senses and powers of Perception. The senses of Sight and Hearing, the two latest in the scale of Evolutionary growth and unfoldment, must receive a particular degree of attention. The student must make himself "aware" of what is going on about and around him, so that he may "catch" the best vibrations.

It would surprise many Westerners if they could come in contact with a highly developed Yogi, and witness the marvelously finely developed senses he possesses. He is able to distinguish the finest differences in things, and his mind is so trained that, in thought, he may draw conclusions from what he has perceived, in a manner that seems almost "second-sight" to the uninitiated. *In fact, a certain degree of second-sight is possible to one who develops his sense of Sight, under the urge of Attention.* A new world is opened out to such a person. One must learn to master the senses, not only in the direction of being independent of and superior to their urgings, but also in the matter of developing them to a high degree. The development of the physical senses, also has much to do with the development of the "Astral Senses," of which we have spoken in our *Fourteen Lessons,* and of which we may have more to say in the present series. The idea of Raja Yoga is to render the student the possessor of a highly developed Mind, with highly developed instruments with which the mind may work.

In our future lessons we shall give the student many illustrations, directions, and exercises calculated to develop the different faculties of the mind—not only the ordinary faculties of everyday use, but others hidden behind these familiar faculties and senses. Commencing with the next lesson, we shall present a system of exercises, drills, etc., the purpose of which will be the abovementioned development of the faculties of the Mind.

In this lesson we shall not attempt to give specific exercises, but will content ourselves with calling the attention of the student to a few general rules underlying the development of Perception.

GENERAL RULES OF PERCEPTION

The first thing to remember in acquiring the art of Perception is that one should not attempt to perceive the whole of a complex thing or object at the same time, or at once. One should consider the object in detail, and then, by grouping the details, he will find that he has considered the whole. Let us take the face of a person as a familiar object. If one tries to perceive a face as a whole, he will find that he will meet with a certain degree of failure, the impression being indistinct and cloudy, it following, also, that the memory of that face will correspond with the original perception.

But let the observer consider the face in detail, first the eyes, then the nose, then the mouth, then the chin, then the hair, then the outline of the face, the complexion, etc., and he will find that he will have acquired a clear and distinct impression or perception of the whole face.

The same rule may be applied to any subject or object. Let us take another familiar illustration. You wish to observe a building. If you simply get a general perception of the building as a whole, you will be able to remember very little about it, except its general outlines, shape, size, color, etc. And a description will prove to be very disappointing. But if you have noted, *in detail*, the material used, the shape of the doors, chimney, roof, porches, decorations, trimmings, ornamentation, size and number of the windowpanes etc., etc., the shape and angles of the roof, etc., you will have an *intelligent* idea of the building, in the place of a mere general outline or impression of such as might be acquired by an animal in passing.

We will conclude this lesson with an anecdote of the methods of that famous naturalist Agassiz, in his training of his pupils. His pupils became renowned for their close powers of observation and perception, and their consequent ability to "think" about the things they had seen. Many of them rose to eminent positions, and claimed that this was largely by reason of their careful training.

The tale runs that a new student presented himself to Agassiz one day, asking to be set to work. The naturalist took a fish from a jar in which it had been preserved, and laying it before the young student bade him observe it carefully, and be ready to report upon what he had noticed about the fish. The student was then left alone with the fish. There was nothing especially interesting about that fish—it was like many other fishes that he had seen before. He noticed that it had fins and scales, and a mouth and eyes, yes, and a tail. In a half hour he felt certain that he had observed all about that fish that there was to be perceived. But the naturalist remained away.

The time rolled on, and the youth, having nothing else to do, began to grow restless and weary. He started out to hunt up the teacher, but he failed to find him, and so had to return and gaze again at that wearisome fish. Several hours had passed, and he knew but little more about the fish than he did in the first place.

He went out to lunch and when he returned it was still a case of watching the fish. He felt disgusted and discouraged, and wished he had never come to Agassiz, whom, it seemed, was a stupid old man after all—one away behind the times. Then, in order to kill time, he began to count the scales. This completed he counted the spines of the fins. Then he began to draw a picture of the fish. In drawing the picture he noticed that the fish had no eyelids. He thus made the discovery that as his teacher had expressed it often, in lectures, "a pencil is the best of eyes." Shortly after the teacher returned, and after ascertaining what the youth had observed, he left rather disappointed, telling the boy to keep on looking and maybe he would see something.

This put the boy on his mettle, and he began to work with his pencil, putting down little details that had escaped him before, but which now seemed very plain to him. He began to catch the secret of observation. Little by little he brought to light new objects of interest about the fish. But this did not suffice his teacher, who kept him at work on the same fish for three whole days. At the end of that time the student really knew something about the fish, and, better than all, had acquired the "knack" and habit of careful observation and perception in detail.

Years after, the student, then attained to eminence, is reported as saying: "That was the best zoological lesson I ever had—a lesson whose influence has extended to the details of every subsequent study; a legacy that the professor left to me, as he left to many others, of inestimable value, which we could not buy, and with which we cannot part."

Apart from the value to the student of the particular information obtained, was the quickening of the perceptive faculties that enabled him to observe the important points in a subject or object, and, consequently to deduce important information from that which was observed. The Mind is hungry for knowledge, and it has by years of weary evolution and effort built up a series of sense systems in order to yield it that knowledge and it is still building. The men and women in the world who have arrived at the point of success have availed themselves of these wonderful channels of information, and by directing them under the guidance of Will and Attention, have attained wonderful results. These things are of importance, and we beg of our students not to pass by this portion of the subject as uninteresting. Cultivate a spirit of wide-awakeness and perception, and the "knowing" that will come to you will surprise you.

Not only do you develop the existing senses by such practice and use, *but you help in the unfoldment of the latent powers and senses that are striving for unfoldment.* By using and exercising the faculties that we have, we help to unfold those for the coming of which we have been dreaming.

SIXTH LESSON—MANTRAM

I am a Soul, possessed of channels of communication
with the outer world. I will use these channels, and
thereby acquire the information and knowledge
necessary for my mental development. I will exercise and
develop my organs of sense, knowing that in so doing I
shall cause to unfold the higher senses, of which they
are but forerunners and symbols. I will be *"wide-awake"*
and open to the inflow of knowledge and information.
The Universe is my Home—I will explore it.

The Unfoldment of Consciousness

We have thought it well to make a slight change in the arrangement of these lessons—that is, in the order in which
they should appear. We had contemplated making this Seventh Lesson a series of Mental Drills, intended to develop
certain of the mental faculties, but we have decided to postpone the same until a later lesson, believing that by so doing a more logical sequence or order of arrangement will be
preserved. In this lesson we will tell you of the unfoldment
of consciousness in Man, and in the next lesson, and probably in the one following it, we shall present to you a clear
statement regarding the states of mind, below and over consciousness—a most wonderful region, we assure you, and
one that has been greatly misunderstood and misinterpreted. This will lead up to the subject of the cultivation of the
various faculties—both conscious and outside of consciousness, and the series will be concluded by three lessons going
right to the heart of this part of the subject, and giving certain rules and instruction calculated to develop Man's won-

derful "thought-machine" that will be of the greatest interest and importance to all of our students. When the lessons are concluded you will see that the present arrangement is most logical and proper.

In this lesson we take up the subject of "The Unfoldment of Consciousness"—a most interesting subject. Many of us have been in the habit of identifying "consciousness" with mind, but as we proceed with this series of lessons we will see that that which is called "consciousness" is but a small portion of the mind of the individual, and even that small part is constantly changing its states, and unfolding new states undreamed of.

"Consciousness" is a word we use very often in considering the science of the Mind. Let us see what it means. Webster defines it as one's "knowledge of sensations and mental operations, or of what passes in one's own mind." Halleck defines it as "that undefinable characteristic of mental states which causes one to be aware of them." But, as Halleck states, "Consciousness is incapable of definition. To define anything we are obliged to describe it in terms of something else. And there is nothing else in the world like consciousness, hence we can define it only in terms of itself, and that is very much like trying to lift one's self by one's own bootstraps. Consciousness is one of the greatest mysteries that confronts us."

Before we can understand what Consciousness really is, we must know just what "Mind" really is—and that knowledge is lacking, notwithstanding the many ingenious theories evolved in order to explain the mystery. The metaphysicians do not throw much light on the subject, and as for materialistic science, listen to what Huxley says: "How it comes about that anything so remarkable as a state of consciousness comes about by the result of irritating nervous tissue, is just as unaccountable as the appearance of the genie when Aladdin rubbed his lamp."

To many persons the words "consciousness" and "mental process," or "thought" are regarded as synonymous. And, in fact, psychologists so held until quite recently. But now it is generally accepted as a fact that mental processes are not limited to the field of consciousness, and it is now generally taught that the field of subconsciousness (that is, "under" conscious) mentation, is of a much greater extent than that of conscious mentation.

Not only is it true that the mind can hold in consciousness but one fact at any one instant, and that, consequently, only a very small fraction of our knowledge can be in consciousness at any one moment, but it is also true that the consciousness plays but a very small part in the totality of mental processes, or mentation. The mind is not conscious of the greater portion of its own activities—Maudsley says that only ten percent comes into the field of consciousness. Taine has stated it in these words: "Of the world which makes up our being, we only perceive the highest points—the lighted up peaks of a continent whose lower levels remain in the shade."

But it is not our intention to speak of this great subconscious region of the mind at this point, for we shall have much to do with it later on. It is mentioned here in order to show that the enlargement or development of consciousness is not so much a matter of "growth" as it is an "unfoldment"—not a new creation or enlargement from outside, but rather an unfoldment outward from within.

From the very beginning of Life—among the Particles of Inorganic Substance, may be found traces of something like Sensation, and response thereto. Writers have not cared to give to this phenomenon the name of "sensation," or "sensibility," as the terms savored too much of "senses," and "sense-organs." But Modern Science has not hesitated to bestow the names so long withheld. The most advanced scientific writers do not hesitate to state that in reaction, chemical response, etc., may be seen indications of rudimentary sensation. Haeckel[6] says:

> I cannot imagine the simplest chemical and physical process without attributing the movement of the material particles to unconscious sensation. The idea of Chemical Affinity consists in the fact that the various chemical elements perceive the qualitative differences in other elements and experience 'pleasure' or 'revulsion' at contacts with them, and execute their specific movements on this ground.

He also speaks of the sensitiveness of "plasm," or the substance of "living bodies," as being "only a superior degree of the general irritability of substance.

Chemical reaction, between atoms, is spoken of by chemists as a "sensitive" reaction. Sensitiveness is found even in the Particles of Inorganic Substance, and may be regarded as the first glimmerings of thought. Science recognizes this when it speaks of the unconscious sensation of the Particles as *athesis* or "feeling," and the unconscious Will that responds thereto, as *tropesis*, or "inclination." Haeckel says of this that "Sensation perceives the different qualities of the stimuli, and feeling the quantity," and also, "We may ascribe the feeling of pleasure and pain (in the contact with qualitatively differing atoms) to all atoms, and so explain the elective affinity in chemistry (attraction of loving atoms, inclination; repulsion of hating atoms, disinclination)."

It is impossible to form a clear or intelligent idea of the

phenomenon of chemical affinity, etc., unless we attribute to the Atoms something akin to Sensation. It is likewise impossible to understand the actions of the Molecules, unless we think of them as possessing something akin to Sensation. The Law of Attraction is based upon Mental States in Substance. The response of Inorganic Substance to Electricity and Magnetism is also another evidence of Sensation and the response thereto.

In the movements and operations of crystal-life we obtain evidences of still a little higher forms of Sensation and response thereto. The action of crystallization is very near akin to that of some low forms of plasmic action. In fact, the "missing link" between plant life and the crystals is claimed to have been found in some recent discoveries of Science, the connection being found in certain crystals in the interior of plants composed of carbon combinations, and resembling the inorganic crystals in many ways.

Crystals grow along certain lines and forms up to a certain size. Then they begin to form "baby-crystals" on their surfaces, which then take on the growth—the processes being almost analogous to cell-life. Processes akin to fermentation have been detected among chemicals. In many ways it may be seen that the beginning of Mental Life must be looked for among the Minerals and Particles—the latter, be it remembered, composing not only inorganic, but also Organic Substance.

As we advance in the scale of life, we are met with constantly increasing unfoldment of mentation, the simple giving place to the complex manifestations. Passing by the simple vital processes of the monera, or single-celled "things," we notice the higher forms of cell life, with growing sensibility or sensation. Then we come to the cell-groups, in which the individual cells manifest sensation of a kind, coupled with a community-sensation. Food is distinguished, selected and captured, and movements exercised in pursuit of the same. The living thing is beginning to manifest more complex mental states. Then the stage of the lower plants is reached, and we notice the varied phenomena of that region, evidencing an increased sensitiveness, although there are practically no signs of special organs of sense. Then we pass on to the higher plant life, in which begin to manifest certain "sensitive-cells," or groups of such cells, which are rudimentary sense organs. Then the forms of animal life, and considered with rising degrees of sensations and growing sense apparatus, or sense organs, gradually unfolding into something like nervous systems.

Among the lower animal forms there are varying degrees of mentation with accompanying nerve centers and sense-organs, but little or no signs of consciousness, gradually ascending until we have dawning consciousness in the reptile kingdom, etc., and fuller consciousness and a degree of intelligent thought in the still higher forms, gradually increasing until we reach the plane of the highest mammals, such as the horse, dog, elephant, ape, etc., which animals have complex nervous systems, brains and well-developed consciousness. We need not further consider the forms of mentation in the forms of life below the Conscious stage, for that would carry us far from our subject.

Among the higher forms of animal life, after a "dawn period" or semiconsciousness, we come to forms of life among the lower animals possessing a well-developed degree of mental action and Consciousness, the latter being called by psychologists "Simple Consciousness," but which term we consider too indefinite, and which we will term "Physical

Consciousness," which will give a fair idea of the thing itself. We use the word "Physical" in the double sense of "External," and "Relating to the material structure of a living being," both of which definitions are found in the dictionaries. And that is just what Physical Consciousness really is—an "awareness" in the mind, or a "consciousness" of the "external" world as evidenced by the senses; and of the "body" of the animal or person. The animal or person thinking on the plane of Physical Consciousness (all the higher animals do, and many men seem unable to rise much higher) identifies itself with the physical body, and is conscious only of thoughts of that body and the outside world. It "knows," but not being conscious of mental operations, or of the existence of its mind, it does not "know that it knows." This form of consciousness, while infinitely above the mentation of the nonconscious plane of "sansation," is like a different world of thought from the consciousness of the highly developed intellectual man of our age and race.

It is difficult for a man to form an idea of the Physical Consciousness of the lower animals and savages, particularly as he finds it difficult to understand his own consciousness except by the act of being conscious. But observation and reason have given us a fair degree of understanding of what this Physical Consciousness of the animal is like—or at least in what respect it differs from our own consciousness. Let us take a favorite illustration. A horse standing out in the cold sleet and rain undoubtedly *feels* the discomfort, and possibly pain, for we know by observation that animals feel both. But he is not able to analyze his mental states and wonder when his master will come out to him—think how cruel it is to keep him out of the warm stable—wonder whether he will be taken out in the cold again tomorrow—feel envious of other horses who are indoors—wonder why he is compelled to be out cold nights, etc., etc.—in short, he does not think as would a reasoning man under such circumstances. He is aware of the discomfort, just as would be the man—and he would run home if he could just as would the man. But he is not able to pity himself, nor to think about his personality as would the man, nor does he wonder whether such a life is worth living, after all. He "knows," but is not able to think of himself as knowing—he does not "know that he knows," as we do. He experiences the physical pain and discomfort, but is spared the mental discomfort and concern arising from the physical, which man so often experiences.

The animal cannot shift its consciousness from the sensations of the outer world to the inner states of being. It is not able to "know itself." The difference may be clumsily illustrated by the example of a man feeling, seeing or hearing something that gives him a pleasurable sensation, or the reverse. He is conscious of the feeling or sensation, and that it is pleasurable or otherwise. That is Physical Consciousness, and the animal may share it with him. But it stops right there with the animal. But the man may begin to wonder *why* the sensation is pleasurable and to associate it with other things and persons; or speculate *why* he dislikes it, what will follow, and so on—that is Mental Consciousness, because he recognizes an inward self, and is turning his attention *inward*. He may see another man and experience a feeling or sensation of attraction or aversion—like or dislike. This is Physical Consciousness, and an animal also may experience the sensation. But the man goes further than the animal, and wonders just what there is about the man he likes or detests, and may compare himself to the man and wonder whether the latter feels as he does, and so on—this is Mental Consciousness.

In animals the mental gaze is freely directed outward, and never returns upon itself. In man the mental gaze may be directed inward, or may return inward after its outward journey. The animal "knows"—the man not only "knows," but he "knows that he knows," and is able to investigate that "knowing" and speculate about it. We call this higher consciousness Mental Consciousness. The operation of Physical Consciousness we call Instinct—the operation of Mental Consciousness we call Reason.

The Man who has Mental Consciousness not only "feels" or "senses" things, but he has words or mental concepts of these feelings and sensations and may think of himself as experiencing them, separating himself, the sensation or feeling, and the thing felt or sensed. The man is able to think: "I feel; I hear; I see; I smell; I taste; I desire; I do," etc., etc. The very words indicate Mental Consciousness recognizing mental states and giving them names, and also recognizing something called "I" that experiences the sensations. This latter fact has caused psychologists to speak of this stage as "Self-consciousness," but we reserve this idea of the "I" consciousness for a higher stage.

The animal experiences something that gives it the impressions or feeling that we call "pain," "hurt," "pleasant," "sweet," "bitter," etc., all being forms of sensation, but it is unable to think of them in words. The pain seems to be a part of itself, although possibly associated with some person or thing that caused it. The study of the unfoldment of consciousness in a young baby will give one a far better idea of the grades and distinctions than can be obtained from reading mere words.

Mental Consciousness is a growth. As Halleck says, "Many persons never have more than a misty idea of such a mental attitude. They always take themselves for granted, and never turn the gaze inward." It has been doubted whether the savages have developed Self-consciousness, and even many men of our own race seem to be but little above the animals in intellect and consciousness. They do not seem able to "know themselves" even slightly. To them the "I" seems to be a purely physical thing—a body having desires and feeling but little more. They are able to feel an act, but scarcely more. They are not able to set aside any physical "not-I," being utterly unable to think of themselves as anything else but a Body. The "I" and the Body are one with them, and they seem incapable of distinguishing between them.

Then comes another stage in which mental-consciousness proper sets in. The man begins to realize that he has "a mind." He is able to "know himself" as a mental being, and to turn the gaze inward a little. This period of development may be noticed in young children. For a time they speak of themselves as a third person, until finally they begin to say "I." Then a little later comes the ability to know their own mental states as such—they know that they have a mind, and are able to distinguish between it and the body. It is related that some children experience a feeling of terror when they pass into this stage. They exhibit signs of bashfulness and what is commonly termed "self-consciousness" in that sense. Some tell us in after years that when they became aware of themselves as an entity they were overcome with alarm, as if by a sense of loneliness and apartness from the Universe. Young people often feel this way for several years. There seems to be a distinct feeling that the Universe is antagonistic to and set apart from them.

And, although this feeling of separateness and apartness grows less acute as the man grows older, yet it is always present to a greater or less degree until a still higher stage—the Ego-consciousness is reached, when it disappears as we shall see. And this mental-conscious stage is a hard one for many. They are entangled in a mass of mental states which the man thinks is "himself," and the struggle between the real "I" and its confining sheaths is painful. And it becomes still more painful as the end is neared, for as man advances in mental-consciousness and knowledge he feels more keenly and suffers accordingly. Man eats the fruit of the Tree of Knowledge and begins to suffer, and is driven out of the Garden of Eden of the child and primitive races, who live like the birds of the air and concern themselves not about mental states and problems. But there is deliverance ahead in the shape of a higher consciousness, although but few realize it and still fewer have gained it. Perhaps this lesson may point out the way for you.

With the birth of mental-consciousness comes the knowledge that there is a mind in others. Man is able to speculate and reason about the mental states of other men, because he recognizes these states within himself. As man advances in the Mental Consciousness he begins to develop a constantly increasing degree and grade of Intellect, and accordingly he attaches the greatest importance to that part of his nature. Some men worship Intellect as a God, ignoring its limitations which other thinkers have pointed out. Such people are apt to reason that because the human intellect (in its present state of development) reports that such a thing *must* be, or *cannot* possibly be, that the matter is forever settled. They ignore the fact that it is possible that Man's Intellect, in its present state of unfoldment, may be able to take cognizance of only a very small part of the Universal Fact, and that there may be regions upon regions of Reality and Fact of which he cannot even dream, so far are they removed from his experience. The unfoldment of a new sense would open out a new world and might bring to light facts that would completely revolutionize our entire world of conceptions by reason of the new information it would give us.

But, nevertheless, from this Mental Consciousness has come the wonderful work of Intellect, as shown in the achievements of Man up to this time, and while we must recognize its limitations, we gladly join in singing its praises. Reason is the tool with which Man is digging into the mine of Facts, bringing to light new treasures every day. This stage of Mental Consciousness is bringing to Man knowledge of himself—knowledge of the Universe—that is well worth the price he pays for it. For Man *does* pay a price for entrance into this stage—and he pays an increasing price as he advances in its territory, for the higher he advances the more keenly he feels and suffers, as well as enjoys. Capacity for pain is the price Man pays for Attainment, up to a certain stage. His pain passes from the Physical to the Mental consciousness, and he becomes aware of problems that he never dreamt existed, and the lack of an intelligent answer produces mental suffering. And the mental suffering that comes to him from unsatisfied longings, disappointment, the pain of others whom he loves, etc., is far worse than any physical suffering.

The animal lives its animal life and is contented, for it knows no better. If it has enough to eat—a place to sleep—a mate—it is happy. And some men are likewise. But others find themselves involved in a world of mental discomfort. New wants arise, and the lack of satisfaction brings pain. Civilization becomes more and more complex, and brings its new pains as well as new pleasures. Man attaches himself to "things," and each day creates for himself artificial wants, which he must labor to meet. His Intellect may not lead him upward, but instead may merely enable him to invent new and subtle means and ways of gratifying his senses to a degree impossible to the animals. Some men make a religion of the gratification of their sensuality—their appetites—and become beasts magnified by the power of Intellect. Others become vain, conceited and puffed up with a sense of the importance of their Personality (the false "I"). Others become morbidly introspective, and spend their time analyzing and dissecting their moods, motives, feelings, etc. Others exhaust their capacity for pleasure and happiness, but looking outside for it instead of within, and become *blasé*, bored, *ennuied* and an affliction to themselves We mention these things not in a spirit of Pessimism but merely to show that even this great Mental Consciousness has a reverse and ugly side as well as the bright face that has been ascribed to it.

As man reaches the higher stages of this Mental Consciousness, and the next higher stage begins to dawn upon him, he is apt to feel more keenly than ever the insufficiency of Life as it appears to him. He is unable to understand Himself—his origin, destiny, purpose and nature—and he chafes against the bars of the cage of Intellect in which he is confined. He asks himself the question, "Whence come I—Whither go I—What is the object of my Existence?" He becomes dissatisfied with the answers the world has to give him to these questions, and he cries aloud in despair—and but the answer of his own voice comes back to him from the impassable walls with which he is surrounded. He does not realize that his answer must come from Within—but so it is.

Psychology stops when it reaches the limits of Mental Consciousness, or as it calls it "Self-Consciousness," and denies that there is anything beyond—any unexplored regions of the Mind. It laughs at the reports that come from those who have penetrated further within the recesses of their being, and dismisses the reports as mere "dreams," "fantasies," "illusions," "ecstatic imaginings," "abnormal states," etc., etc. But, nevertheless, there are schools of thought that teach of these higher states, and there are men of all ages and races that have entered them and have reported concerning them. And we feel justified in asking you to take them into consideration.

There are two planes of Consciousness, of which we feel it proper to speak, for we have obtained more or less information regarding them. There are still higher planes, but they belong to higher phases of life than are dealt with here.

The first of these planes or states of Consciousness, above the "Self-Consciousness" of the psychologists (which we have called "Mental Consciousness") may be called "Ego-consciousness," for it brings an "awareness" of the Reality of the Ego. This "awareness" is far above the Self-consciousness of the man who is able to distinguish "I" from "You," and to give it a name. And far above the consciousness that enables a man, as he rises in the scale, to distinguish the "I" from faculty after faculty of the mind, which he is able to recognize as "not-I," until he finds left a mental something that he cannot set aside, which he calls "I"— although this stage alone is very much higher than that of the average of the race, and is a high degree of Attainment itself. It is akin to this last stage, and yet still fuller and more complete. In the dawning of Ego Consciousness the "I" recognizes itself still more clearly and, more than this, is fully imbued with a sense and "awareness" of its own *Reality*, unknown to it before. This awareness is not a mere matter of reasoning— it is a "consciousness," just as is Physical Consciousness and

Mental Consciousness something different from an "intellectual conviction." It is a Knowing, not a Thinking or Believing. The "I" *knows* that it is Real—that it has its roots in the Supreme Reality underlying all the Universe, and partakes of its Essence. It does not know what this Reality is, but it knows that it is Real, and something different from anything in the world of name, form, number, time, space, cause and effect—something Transcendental and surpassing all human experience. And knowing this, it knows that it cannot be destroyed or hurt; cannot die, but is immortal; and that there is Something which is the very essence of Good behind of, underneath and even *in* itself. And in this certainty and consciousness is there Peace, Understanding and Power. When it fully bursts upon one, Doubt, Fear, Unrest and Dissatisfaction drop from him like worn-out garments and he finds himself clothed in the Faith that Knows; Fearlessness; Restfulness; Satisfaction. Then he is able to say understandingly and with meaning "I AM."

This Ego Consciousness is coming to many as a dawning knowledge—the light is just rising from behind the hills. To others it has come gradually and slowly, but fully, and they now live in the full light of the consciousness. Others it has burst upon like a flash, or vision—like a light falling from the clear sky, almost blinding them at first, but leaving them changed men and women, possessed of that something that cannot be understood by or described to those who have not experienced it. This last stage is called "Illumination" in one of its forms.

The man of the Ego Consciousness may not understand the Riddle of the Universe or be able to give an answer to the great Questions of Life—but he has ceased to worry about them—they now disturb him not. He may use his intellect upon them as before, but never with the feeling that in their intellectual solution rests his happiness or peace of mind. He knows that he stands on solid rock, and though the storms of the world of matter and force may beat upon him, he will not be hurt. This and other things he knows. He cannot prove these things to others, for they are not demonstrable by argument—he himself did not get them in that way. And so he says but little about it—but lives his life as if he knew them not, so far as outward appearances go. But inwardly he is a changed man—his life is different from that of his brothers, for while their souls are wrapped in slumber or are tossing in troubled dreams, his Soul has awakened and is gazing upon the world with bright and fearless eyes. There are, of course, different stages or degrees of this Consciousness, just as there are in the lower planes of consciousness. Some have it to a slight degree, while others have it fully. Perhaps this lesson will tell some of its readers just what is the thing that has "happened" to them and which they hesitate to speak of to their closest friend or life companion. To others it may open the way to a fuller realization. We sincerely trust so, for one does not begin to Live until he knows the "I" as Reality.

There is a stage still higher than this last mentioned but it has come to but very few of the race. Reports of it come from all times, races, countries. It has been called "Cosmic Consciousness," and is described as an awareness of the Oneness of Life—that is, a consciousness that the Universe is filled with One Life—an actual perception and "awareness" that the Universe is full of Life, Motion and Mind, and that there is no such thing as Blind Force, or Dead Matter, but that All is alive, vibrating and intelligent. That is, of course, that the *Real Universe*, which is the Essence or background of the Universe of Matter, Energy and Mind, is as they de-

scribe. In fact, the description of those who have had glimpses of this state would indicate that they see the Universe as
All Mind—that All is Mind at the last. This form of consciousness has been experienced by men here and there—
only a few—in moments of "Illumination," the period lasting
but a very short space of time, then fading away, leaving but
a memory. In the moment of the "Illumination" there came
to those experiencing it a sense of "in-touch-ness" with Universal Knowledge and Life, impossible to describe, accompanied by a Joy beyond understanding.

Regarding this last, "Cosmic Consciousness," we would
state that it means more than an intellectual conviction, belief or realization of the facts as stated, for an actual *vision*
and *consciousness* of these things came in the moment of Illumination. Some others report that they have a deep abid-
ing sense of the reality of the facts described by the report of
the Illumined, but have not experienced the "vision" or ec-
stasy referred to. These last people seem to have with them
always the same mental state as that possessed by those who
had the "vision" and passed out of it, carrying with them the
remembrance and feeling, but not the actual consciousness
attained at the moment. They agree upon the essential particulars of the reports. Dr. Maurice Bucke,[7] now passed out of
this plane of life, wrote a book entitled *Cosmic Consciousness*,
in which he describes a number of these cases, including his
own, Walt Whitman's[8] and others, and in which he holds that
this stage of consciousness is before the race and will gradually come to it in the future. He holds that the manifestation
of it which has come to some few of the race, as above stated,
is but the first beams of the sun which are flashing upon us
and which are but prophecies of the appearance of the great
body of light itself.

We shall not here consider at length the reports of certain great religious personages of the past, who have left records that in moments of great spiritual exaltation they became conscious of "being in the presence of the Absolute," or perhaps within the radius of "the light of Its countenance." We have great respect for these reports, and have every reason for believing many of them authentic, notwithstanding the conflicting reports that have been handed down to us by those experiencing them. These reports are conflicting because of the fact that the minds of those who had these glimpses of consciousness were not prepared or trained to fully understand the nature of the phenomena. They found themselves in the spiritual presence of Something of awful grandeur and spiritual rank, and were completely dazed and bewildered at the sight. They did not understand the nature of the Absolute, and when they had sufficiently recovered they reported that they had been in the "presence of God"— the word "God" meaning their particular conception of Deity—that is, the one appearing as Deity in their own particular religious creed or school. They saw nothing to cause them to identify this Something with their particular conception of Deity, except that they thought that "it *must* be God," and knowing no other God except their own particular conception, they naturally identifying the Something with "God" as they conceived Him to be. And their reports naturally were along these lines.

Thus the reports of all religions are filled with accounts of the so-called miraculous occurrences. The Catholic saint reports that he "saw of light of God's countenance," and the non-Catholic reports likewise regarding God as he knows him. The Mohammedan reports that he caught a glimpse of the face of Allah, and the Buddhist tells us that he saw Buddha under the tree. The Brahman has seen the face of Brahma, and the various Hindu sects have men who give similar reports regarding their own particular deities. The Persians have given similar reports, and even the ancient Egyptians have left records of similar occurrences. These conflicting reports have led to the belief, on the part of those who did not understand the nature of the phenomena, that these things were "all imagination" and fancy, if indeed not rank falsehood and imposture. But the Yogis know better than this. They know that underneath all these varying reports there is a common ground of truth, which will be apparent to anyone investigating the matter. They know that all of these reports (except a few based upon fraudulent imitation of the real phenomenon) are based upon truth and are but the bewildered reports of the various observers. They know that these people were temporarily lifted above the ordinary plane of consciousness and were made aware of the existence of a Being or Beings higher than mortal. It does not follow that they saw "God" or the Absolute, for there are many Beings of high spiritual growth and development that would appear to the ordinary mortal as a very God. The Catholic doctrine of Angels and Archangels is corroborated by those among the Yogis who have been "behind the Veil," and they give us reports of the "Devas" and other advanced Beings. So the Yogi accepts these reports of the various mystics, saints and inspired ones, and accounts for them all by laws perfectly natural to the students of the Yogi Philosophy, but which appear as supernatural to those who have not studied along these lines.

But we cannot speak further of this phase of the subject in this lesson, for a full discussion of it would lead us far away from the phase of the general subject before us. But we wish to be understood as saying that there are certain centers in the mental being of Man from which may come light regarding the existence of the Absolute and higher order of Beings. In fact, from these centers come to man that part of his mental "feelings" that he calls "the religious instinct or intuition." Man does not arrive at that underlying consciousness of "Something Beyond" by means of his Intellect—it is the glimmer of light coming from the higher centers of the Self. He notices these gleams of light, but not understanding them, he proceeds to erect elaborate theological and creedal structures to account for them, the work of the Intellect, however, always lacking that "feeling" that the intuition itself possesses. True religion, no matter under what name it may masquerade, comes from the "heart" and is not comforted or satisfied with these Intellectual explanations, and hence comes that unrest and craving for satisfaction which comes to Man when the light begins to break through.

But we must postpone a further discussion of this part of the subject for the present. We shall consider it again in a future lesson in connection with other matters. As we have said, our next two lessons will take upon the inquiry regarding the regions outside of the consciousness of the ordinary man. You will find it a most fascinating and instructive inquiry and one that will open up new fields of thought for many of you.

SEVENTH LESSON—MANTRAM

I Am a Being far greater and grander than
I have as yet conceived. I am unfolding
gradually but surely into higher planes of
consciousness. I am moving Forward and
Upward constantly. My goal is the Realization
of the True Self, and I welcome each stage
of Unfoldment that leads me toward my aim.
I am a manifestation of REALITY.
I *AM*.

The Highlands and Lowlands of Mind

The Self of each of us has a vehicle of expression which we call the Mind, but which vehicle is much larger and far more complex than we are apt to realize. As a writer has said "Our Self is greater than we know; it has peaks above, and lowlands below the plateau of our conscious experience." That which we know as the "conscious mind" is not the Soul. The Soul is not a part of that which we know in consciousness, but, on the contrary, that which we know in consciousness is but a small part of the Soul—the conscious vehicle of a greater Self, or "I."

The Yogis have always taught that the mind has many planes of manifestation and action—and that many of its planes operated above and below the plane of consciousness. Western science is beginning to realize this fact, and its theories regarding the same may be found in any of the later works on psychology. But this is a matter of recent development in Western science. Until very recently the textbooks held that Consciousness and Mind were synonymous, and that the Mind was conscious of all of its activities, changes and modifications.

Leibniz was one of the first Western philosophers to advance the idea that there were planes of mental activity outside of the plane of consciousness, and since his time the leading thinkers have slowly but surely moved forward to his position.

At the present time it is generally conceded that at least ninety percent of our mental operations take place in the out-of-conscious realm. Prof. Elmer Gates, the well-known scientist, has said:

> At least ninety percent of our mental life is subconscious. If you will analyze your mental operations you will find that conscious thinking is never a continuous line of consciousness, but a series of conscious data with great intervals of subconscious. We sit and try to solve a problem, and fail. We walk around, try again, and fail. Suddenly an idea dawns that leads to the solution of the problem. The subconscious processes were at work. We do not volitionally create our own thinking. It takes place in us. We are more or less passive recipients. We cannot change the nature of a thought, or of a truth, but we can, as it were, *guide the ship by a moving of the helm.* Our mentation is largely the result of the great Cosmic Whole upon us.

Sir William Hamilton says that the sphere of our consciousness is only a small circle in the center of a far wider sphere of action and thought, of which we are conscious through its effects.

Taine says: "Outside of a little luminous circle, lies a large ring of twilight, and beyond this an indefinite night; but the events of this twilight and this night are as real as those within the luminous circle."

Sir Oliver Lodge, the eminent English scientist, speaking of the planes of the mind, says:

> Imagine an iceberg glorying in its crisp solidity, and sparkling pinnacles, resenting attention paid to its submerged self, or supporting region, or to the saline liquid out of which it arose, and into which in due course it will someday return. Or, reversing the metaphor, we might liken our present state to that of the hulls of ships submerged in a dim ocean among strange monsters, propelled in a blind manner through space; proud perhaps of accumulating many barnacles as decoration; only recognizing our destination by bumping against the dock-wall; and with no cognizance of the deck and cabins above us, or the spars and sails—no thought of the sextant, and the compass, and the captain—no perception of the lookout on the mast—of the distant horizon. With no vision of objects far ahead—dangers to be avoided—destinations to be reached—other ships to be spoken to by means other than by bodily contact—a region of sunshine and cloud, of space, or perception, and of intelligence utterly inaccessible to parts below the waterline.

We ask our students to read carefully the above expression of Sir Oliver Lodge, for it gives one of the clearest and most accurate figures of the actual state of affairs concerning the mental planes that we have seen in Western writings.

And other Western writers have noted and spoken of these out-of-conscious realms. Lewes has said: "It is very certain that in every conscious volition—every act that is so characterized—the larger part of it is quite unconscious. It is equally certain that in every perception there are unconscious processes of reproduction and inference. There is a middle distance of subconsciousness, and a background of unconsciousness."

Taine has told us that: "Mental events imperceptible to consciousness are far more numerous than the others, and of the world that makes up our being we only perceive the highest points—the lighted-up peaks of a continent whose lower levels remain in the shade. Beneath ordinary sensations are their components, that is to say, the elementary sensations, which must be combined into groups to reach our consciousness."

Maudsley says: "Examine closely and without bias the ordinary mental operations of daily life, and you will find that consciousness has not one-tenth part of the function therein which it is commonly assumed to have. In every conscious state there are at work conscious, subconscious, and infra-conscious energies, the last as indispensable as the first."

Oliver Wendall Holmes[9] said: "There are thoughts that never emerge into consciousness, which yet make their influence felt among the perceptible mental currents, just as the unseen planets sway the movements of those that are watched and mapped by the astronomer."

Many other writers have given us examples and instances of the operation of the out-of-consciousness planes of thought. One has written that when the solution of a problem he had long vainly dealt with, flashed across his mind, he trembled as if in the presence of another being who had communicated a secret to him. All of us have tried to remember a name or similar thing without success, and have then dismissed the matter from our minds, only to have the missing name or thought suddenly presented to our conscious mind a few minutes, or hours, afterwards. Something in our mind was at work hunting up the missing word, and when it found it it presented it to us.

A writer has mentioned what he called "unconscious rumination," which happened to him when he read books presenting new points of view essentially opposed to his previous opinions. After days, weeks, or months, he found that to his great astonishment the old opinions were entirely rearranged, and new ones lodged there. Many examples of this unconscious mental digestion and assimilation are mentioned in the books on the subject written during the past few years.

It is related of Sir W. R. Hamilton that he discovered quaternions one day while walking with his wife in the observatory at Dublin. He relates that he suddenly felt "the galvanic circle of thought" close, and the sparks that fell from it was the fundamental mathematical relations of his problem, which is now an important law in mathematics.

Dr. Thompson has written:

At times I have had a feeling of the uselessness of all voluntary effort, and also that the matter was working itself clear in my mind. It has many times seemed to me that I was really a passive instrument in the hands of a person not myself. In view of having to wait for the results of these unconscious processes, I have proved the habit of getting together material in advance, and then leaving the mass to digest itself till I am ready to write about it. I delayed for a month the writing of my book *System of Psychology*, but continued reading the authorities. I would not try to think about the book. I would watch with interest the people passing the windows. One evening when reading the paper, the substance of the missing part of the book flashed upon my mind, and I began to write. This is only a sample of many such experiences.

Berthelot, the founder of Synthetic Chemistry, has said that the experiments leading to his wonderful discoveries have never been the result of carefully followed trains of thought—of pure reasoning processes—but have come of themselves, so to speak, from the clear sky.

Mozart has written: "I cannot really say that I can account for my compositions. My ideas flow, and I cannot say whence or how they come. I do not hear in my imagination the parts successively, but I hear them, as it were, all at once. The rest is merely an attempt to reproduce what I have heard."

Dr. Thompson, abovementioned, has also said: "In writing this work I have been unable to arrange my knowledge of a subject for days and weeks, until I experienced a clearing up of my mind, when I took my pen and unhesitatingly wrote the result. I have best accomplished this by leading the (conscious) mind as far away as possible from the subject upon which I was writing."

Prof. Barrett says: "The mysteriousness of our being is not confined to subtle physiological processes which we have in common with all animal life. There are higher and more capacious powers wrapped up in our human personality than are expressed even by what we know of consciousness, will, or reason. There are supernormal and transcendental powers of which, at present, we only catch occasional glimpses; and behind and beyond the supernormal there are fathomless abysses, the Divine ground of the soul; the ultimate reality of which our consciousness is but the reflection or faint perception. Into such lofty themes I do not propose to enter, they must be forever beyond the scope of human inquiry; nor is it possible within the limits of this paper to give any adequate conception of those mysterious regions of our complex personality, which are open to, and beginning to be disclosed by, scientific investigation."

Rev. Dr. Andrew Murray has written: "Deeper down than where the soul with its consciousness can enter there is spirit matter linking man with God; and deeper down than the mind and feelings or will—in the unseen depths of the hidden life—there dwells the Spirit of God." This testimony is remarkable, coming from that source, for it corroborates and reiterates the Yogi teachings of the Indwelling Spirit.

Schofield has written:

Our conscious mind as compared with the unconscious mind, has been likened to the visible spectrum of the sun's rays, as compared to the invisible part which stretches indefinitely on either side. We know now that the chief part of heat comes from the ultrared rays that show no light; and the main part of the chemical changes in the vegetable world are the results of the ultraviolet rays at the other end of the spectrum, which are equally invisible to the eye, and are recognized only by their potent effects. Indeed as these invisible rays extend indefinitely on both sides of the visible spectrum, so we may say that the mind includes not only the visible or conscious part, and what we have termed the subconscious, that which lies below the red line, but the supraconscious mind that lies at the other end—all those regions of higher soul and spirit life, of which we are only at times vaguely conscious, but which always exist, and link us on to eternal verities, on the one side, as surely as the subconscious mind links us to the body on the other.

We know that our students will appreciate the above testimony of Dr. Schofield, for it is directly in the line of our teachings in the Yogi Philosophy regarding the Planes of the Mind (see *Fourteen Lessons*).

We feel justified in quoting further from Dr. Schofield, for he voices in the strongest manner that which the Yogi Philosophy teaches as fundamental truths regarding the mind. Dr. Schofield is an English writer on Psychology, and so far as we know has no tendency toward occultism, his views having been arrived at by careful scientific study and investigation along the lines of Western psychology, which renders his testimony all the more valuable, showing as it does, how the human mind will instinctively find its way to the Truth, even if it has to blaze a new trail through the woods, departing from the beaten tracks of other minds around it, which lack the courage or enterprise to strike out for themselves.

Dr. Schofield writes: "The mind, indeed, reaches all the way, and while on the one hand it is inspired by the Almighty, on the other it energizes the body, all whose purposive life it originates. We may call the supraconscious mind the sphere of the spirit life, the subconscious the sphere of the body life, and the conscious mind the middle region where both meet."

Continuing, Dr. Schofield says: "The Spirit of God is said to dwell in believers, and yet, as we have seen, His presence is not the subject of direct consciousness. We would include, therefore, in the supraconscious, all such spiritual ideas, together with conscience—the voice of God, as Max Müller calls it—which is surely a half-conscious faculty. Moreover, the supraconscious, like the subconscious, is, as we have said, best apprehended when the conscious mind is not active. Visions, meditations, prayers, and even dreams have been undoubtedly occasions of spiritual revelations, and many instances may be adduced as illustrations of the workings of the Spirit apart from the action of reason or mind. The truth apparently is that the mind as a whole is an unconscious state, by that its middle registers, excluding the highest spiritual and lowest physical manifestations, are fitfully illuminated in varying degree by consciousness; and that it is to this illuminated part of the dial that the word 'mind,' which rightly appertains to the whole, has been limited."

Oliver Wendell Holmes has said: "The automatic flow of thought is often singularly favored by the fact of listening to a weak continuous discourse, with just enough ideas in it to keep the (conscious) mind busy. The induced current of thought is often rapid and brilliant in inverse ratio to the force of the inducing current."

Wundt says: "The unconscious logical processes are carried on with a certainty and regularity which would be impossible where there exists the possibility of error. Our mind is so happily designed that it prepares for us the most important foundations of cognition, whilst we have not the slightest apprehension of the *modus operandi*. This unconscious soul, like a benevolent stranger, works and makes provisions for our benefit, pouring only the mature fruits into our laps."

A writer in an English magazine interestingly writes: "Intimations reach our consciousness from unconsciousness, that the mind is ready to work, is fresh, is full of ideas." "The grounds of our judgment are often knowledge so remote from consciousness that we cannot bring them to view." "That the human mind includes an unconscious part; that unconscious events occurring in that part are proximate causes of consciousness; that the greater part of human intuitional action is an effect of an unconscious cause; the truth of these propositions is so deducible from ordinary mental events, and is so near the surface that the failure of deduction to forestall induction in the discerning of it may well excite wonder." "Our behavior is influenced by unconscious assumptions respecting our own social and intellectual rank, and that of the one we are addressing. In company we unconsciously assume a bearing quite different from that of the home circle. After being raised to a higher rank the whole behavior subtly and unconsciously changes in accordance with it." And Schofield adds to the last sentence: "This is also the case in a minor degree with different styles and qualities of dress and different environments. Quite unconsciously we change our behavior, carriage, and style, to suit the circumstance."

Jensen writes: "When we reflect on anything with the whole force of the mind, we may fall into a state of entire unconsciousness, in which we not only forget the outer world, but also know nothing at all of ourselves and the thoughts passing within us after a time. We then suddenly awake as from a dream, and usually at the same moment the result of our meditations appears as distinctly in consciousness without our knowing how we reached it."

Bascom says: "It is inexplicable how premises which lie below consciousness can sustain conclusions in consciousness; how the mind can wittingly take up a mental movement at an advanced stage, having missed its primary steps."

Hamilton and other writers have compared the mind's action to that of a row of billiard balls, of which one is struck and the impetus transmitted throughout the entire row, the result being that only the last ball actually moves, the others remaining in their places. The last ball represents the conscious thought—the other stages in the unconscious mentation. Lewes, speaking of this illustration, says: "Something like this, Hamilton says, seems often to occur in a train of thought, one idea immediately suggesting another into consciousness—this suggestion passing through one or more ideas which do not themselves rise into consciousness. This point, that we are not conscious of the formation of groups, but only of a formed group, may throw light on the existence of unconscious judgments, unconscious reasonings, and unconscious registrations of experience."

Many writers have related the process by which the unconscious mentation emerges gradually into the field of consciousness, and the discomfort attending the process. A few examples may prove interesting and instructive.

Maudsley says: "It is surprising how uncomfortable a person may be made by the obscure idea of something which he ought to have said or done, and which he cannot for the life of him remember. There is an effort of the lost idea to get into consciousness, which is relieved directly the idea bursts into consciousness."

Oliver Wendell Holmes said: "There are thoughts that never emerge into consciousness, and which yet make their influence felt among the perceptive mental currents, just as the unseen planets sway the movements of the known ones." The same writer also remarks: "I was told of a businessman in Boston who had given up thinking of an important question as too much for him. But he continued so uneasy in his brain that he feared he was threatened with palsy. After some hours the natural solution of the question came to him, worked out, as he believed, in that troubled interval."

Dr. Schofield mentions several instances of this phase of the workings of the unconscious planes of the mind. We mention a couple that seem interesting and to the point:

Last year I was driving to Phillmore Gardens to give some letters to a friend. On the way, a vague uneasiness sprang up, and a voice seemed to say, 'I doubt if you have those letters.' Conscious reason rebuked it, and said, 'Of course you have; you took them out of the drawer specially.' The vague feeling was not satisfied, but could not reply. On arrival I found the letters were in none of my pockets. On returning I found them on the hall table, where they had been placed a moment putting on my gloves.

The other day I had to go to see a patient in Folkestone, in Shakespeare Terrace. I got there very late, and did not stay but drove down to the Pavilion for the night, it being dark and rainy. Next morning at eleven I walked up to find the house, knowing the general direction, though never having walked there before. I went up the main road, and, after passing a certain turning, began to feel a vague uneasiness coming into consciousness, that I had passed the terrace. On asking the way, I found it was so; and the turning was where the uneasiness began. The night before was pitch dark, and very wet, and anything seen from a close carriage was quite unconsciously impressed on my mind.

Prof. Kirchener says: "Our consciousness can only grasp one quite clear idea at once. All other ideas are for the time somewhat obscure. They are really existing, but only potentially for consciousness, *i.e.,* they hover, as it were, on our horizon, or beneath the threshold of consciousness. The fact that former ideas suddenly return to consciousness is simply explained by the fact that they have continued psychic existence: and attention is sometimes voluntarily or involuntarily turned away from the present, and the appearance of former ideas is thus made possible."

Oliver Wendell Holmes says: "Our different ideas are stepping-stones; how we get from one to another we do not know; something carries us. We (our conscious selves) do not take the step. The creating and informing spirit, which is *within* us and not *of* us, is recognized everywhere in real life. It comes to us as a voice that will be heard; it tells us what we must believe; it frames our sentences and we wonder at this visitor who chooses our brain as his dwelling place."

Galton says: "I have desired to show how whole states of mental operation that have lapsed out of ordinary consciousness, admit of being dragged into light."

Montgomery says: "We are constantly aware that feelings emerge unsolicited by any previous mental state, directly from the dark womb of unconsciousness. Indeed all our most vivid feelings are thus mystically derived. Suddenly a new irrelevant, unwilled, unlooked-for presence intrudes itself into consciousness. Some inscrutable power causes it to rise and enter the mental presence as a sensorial constituent. If this vivid dependence on unconscious forces has to be conjectured with regard to the most vivid mental occurrences, how much more must such a sustaining foundation be postulated for those faint revivals of previous sensations that so largely assist in making up our complex mental presence!"

Sir Benjamin Brodie says: "It has often happened to me to have accumulated a store of facts, but to have been able to proceed no further. Then after an interval of time, I have found the obscurity and confusion to have cleared away: the facts to have settled in their right places, though I have not been sensible of having made any effort for that purpose."

Wundt says: "The traditional opinion that consciousness is the entire field of the internal life cannot be accepted.

In consciousness, psychic acts are very distinct from one another, and observation itself necessarily conducts to unity in psychology. But the agent of this unity is outside of consciousness, which knows only the result of the work done in the unknown laboratory beneath it. Suddenly a new thought springs into being. Ultimate analysis of psychic processes shows that the unconscious is the theater of the most important mental phenomena. The conscious is always conditional upon the unconscious."

Creighton says: "Our conscious life is the sum of these entrances and exits. Behind the scenes, as we infer, there lies a vast reserve which we call 'the unconscious,' finding a name for it by the simple device of prefixing the negative article. The basis of all that lies behind the scene is the mere negative of consciousness."

Maudsley says: "The process of reasoning adds nothing to knowledge (in the reasoner). It only displays what was there before, and brings to conscious possession what before was unconscious." And again: "Mind can do its work without knowing it. Consciousness is the light that lightens the process, not the agent that accomplishes it."

Walstein says: "It is through the subconscious self that Shakespeare must have perceived, without effort, great truths which are hidden from the conscious mind of the student; that Phidias painted marble and bronze; that Raphael painted Madonnas, and Beethoven composed symphonies."

Ribot says: "The mind receives from experience certain data, and elaborates them unconsciously by laws peculiar to itself, and the result merges into consciousness."

Newman says: "When the unaccustomed causes surprise, we do not perceive the thing and then feel the surprise; but surprise comes first, and then we search out the cause; so the theory must have acted on the unconscious mind to create the feeling, before being perceived in consciousness."

A writer in an English magazine says: "Of what transcendent importance is the fact that the unconscious part of the mind bears to the conscious part such a relation as the magic lantern bears to the luminous disc which it projects; that the greater part of the intentional action, the whole practical life of the vast majority of men, is an effect of events as remote from consciousness as the motion of the planets."

Dr. Schofield says: "It is quite true that the range of the unconscious mind must necessarily remain indefinite; none can say how high or low it may reach.... As to how far the unconscious powers of life that, as has been said, can make eggs and feathers out of Indian corn, and milk and beef and mutton out of grass, are to be considered within or beyond the lowest limits of unconscious mind, we do not therefore here press. It is enough to establish the fact of its existence; to point out its more important features; and to show that in all respects it is as worthy of being called mind as that which works in consciousness. We therefore return to our first definition of Mind, as 'the sum of psychic action in us, whether conscious or unconscious.'"

Hartmann calls our attention to a very important fact when he says: "The unconscious does not fall ill, the unconscious does not grow weary, but all conscious mental activity becomes fatigued."

Kant says: "To have ideas and yet not be conscious of them—therein seems to lie a contradiction. However, we may still be immediately aware of holding an idea, though we are not directly conscious of it."

Maudsley says: "It may seem paradoxical to assert not

merely that ideas may exist in the mind without any consciousness of them, but that an idea, or a train of associated ideas, may be quickened into action and actuate movements without itself being attended to. When an idea disappears from consciousness it does not necessarily disappear entirely; it may remain latent below the horizon of consciousness. Moreover it may produce an effect upon movement, or upon other ideas, when thus active below the horizon of consciousness."

Leibniz says: "It does not follow that because we do not perceive thought that it does not exist. It is a great source of error to believe that there is no perception in the mind but that of which it is conscious."

Oliver Wendell Holmes says: "The more we examine the mechanism of thought the more we shall see that anterior unconscious action of the mind that enters largely into all of its processes. People who talk most do not always think most. I question whether persons who think most— that is who have most conscious thought pass through their mind—necessarily do most mental work. Every new idea planted in a real thinker's mind grows when he is least conscious of it."

Maudsley says: "It would go hard with mankind indeed, if they must act wittingly before they acted at all. Men, without knowing why, follow a course for which good reasons exist. Nay, more. The practical instincts of mankind often work beneficially in actual contradiction to their professed doctrines."

The same writer says: "The best thoughts of an author are the unwilled thoughts which surprise himself; and the poet, under the influence of creative activity, is, so far as consciousness is concerned, being dictated to."

A writer in an English magazine says: "When waiting on a pier for a steamer, I went on to the first, which was the wrong one. I came back and waited, losing my boat, which was at another part of the pier, on account of the unconscious assumption I had made, that this was the only place to wait for the steamer. I saw a man enter a room, and leave by another door. Shortly after, I saw another man exactly like him do the same. It was the same man; but I said it must be his twin brother, in the unconscious assumption that there was no exit for the first man but by the way he came (that by returning)."

Maudsley says: "The firmest resolve or purpose sometimes vanishes issueless when it comes to the brink of an act, while the true will, which determines perhaps a different act, springs up suddenly out of the depths of the unconscious nature, surprising and overcoming the conscious."

Schofield says: "Our unconscious influence is the projection of our unconscious mind and personality unconsciously over others. This acts unconsciously on their unconscious centers, producing effects in character and conduct, recognized in consciousness. For instance, the entrance of a good man into a room where foul language is used, will unconsciously modify and purify the tone of the whole room. Our minds cast shadows of which we are as unconscious as those cast by our bodies, but which affect for good or evil all who unconsciously pass within their range. This is a matter of daily experience, and is common to all, though more noticeable with strong personalities."

Now we have given much time and space to the expressions of opinion of various Western writers regarding this subject of there being a plane or planes of the mind outside of the field of consciousness. We have given space to this valuable testimony, not alone because of its intrinsic value and merit, but because we wished to impress upon the minds of our students that these out-of-conscious planes of mind are now being recognized by the best authorities in the Western world, although it has been only a few years back when the idea was laughed at as ridiculous, and as a mere "dream of the Oriental teachers." Each writer quoted has brought out some interesting and valuable point of the subject, and the student will find that his own experiences corroborate the points cited by the several writers. In this way we think the matter will be made plainer, and will become fixed in the mind of those who are studying this course of lessons.

But we must caution our students from hastily adopting the several theories of Western writers, advanced during the past few years, regarding these out-of-conscious states. The trouble has been that the Western writers dazzled by the view of the subconscious planes of mentation that suddenly burst upon the Western thought, hastily adopted certain theories, which they felt would account for all the phenomena known as "psychic," and which they thought would fully account for all the problems of the subject. These writers while doing a most valuable work, which has helped thousands to form new ideas regarding the nature and workings of the mind, nevertheless did not sufficiently explore the nature of the problem before them. A little study of the Oriental philosophies might have saved them and their readers much confusion.

For instance, the majority of these writers hastily assumed that because there *was* an out-of-conscious plane of mentation, therefore all the workings of the mind might be grouped under the head of "conscious" and "subconscious," and that all the out-of-conscious phenomena might be grouped under the head of "subconscious mind," "subjective mind," etc., ignoring the fact that this class of mental phenomena embraced not only the highest but the lowest forms of mentation. In their newly found "mind" (which they called "subjective" or "subconscious"), they placed the lowest traits and animal passions; insane impulses; delusions; bigotry; animal-like intelligence, etc., etc., as well as the inspiration of the poet and musician, and the high spiritual longings and feelings that one recognizes as having come from the higher regions of the soul.

This mistake was a natural one, and at first reading the Western world was taken by storm, and accepted the new ideas and theories as Truth. But when reflection came, and analysis was applied there arose a feeling of disappointment and dissatisfaction, and people began to feel that there was something lacking. They intuitively recognized that their higher inspirations and intuitions came from a different part of the mind than the lower emotions, passions, and other subconscious feelings, and instincts.

A glance at the Oriental philosophies will give one the key to the problem at once. The Oriental teachers have always held that the conscious mentation was but a small fraction of the entire volume of thought, but they have always taught that just as there was a field of mentation *below* consciousness, so was there a field of mentation *above* consciousness as much higher than Intellect as the other was lower than it. The mere mention of this fact will prove a revelation to those who have not heard it before, and who have become entangled with the several "dual-mind" theories of the recent Western writers. The more one has read on this subject the more he will appreciate the superiority of the Oriental theory over that of the Western writers. It is like the chemical which at once clears the clouded liquid in the test tube.

In our next lesson we shall go into this subject of the above-conscious planes, and the below-conscious planes, bringing out the distinction clearly, and adding to what we have said on the subject in previous books.

And all this is leading us toward the point where we may give you instruction regarding the training and cultivation—the retraining and guidance of these out-of-conscious faculties. By retraining the lower planes of mentation to their proper work, and by stimulating the higher ones, man may "make himself over." mentally, and may acquire powers of which he but dreams now. This is why we are leading you up to the understanding of this subject, step by step. We advise you to acquaint yourself with each phase of the matter, that you may be able to apply the teachings and instructions to follow in later lessons of the course.

EIGHTH LESSON—MANTRAM

I recognize that my Self is greater than it seems—that above and below consciousness are planes of mind—that just as there are lower planes of mind which belong to my past experience in ages past and over which I must now assert my Mastery—so are there planes of mind into which I am unfolding gradually, which will bring me wisdom, power, and joy. I Am Myself, in the midst of this mental world—I am the Master of my Mind—I assert my control of its lower phases, and I demand of its higher all that it has in store for me.

The Mental Planes

In our last lesson we told you something about the operation of the mind outside of the field of consciousness. In this lesson we will attempt to classify these out-of-consciousness planes, by directing your attention to the several mental planes above and below the plane of consciousness. As we stated in the last lesson, over 90 percent of our mental operations are conducted outside of the field of consciousness, so that the consideration of the planes is seen to be an important subject.

Man is a Centre of Consciousness in the great One Life of the Universe. His soul has climbed a great many steps before it reached its present position and stage of unfoldment. And it will pass through many more steps until it is entirely free and delivered from the necessity of its swaddling clothes.

In his mental being man contains traces of all that has gone before—all the experiences of himself and the great race movement of which he is a part. And, likewise, his mind contains faculties and mental planes which have not as yet unfolded into consciousness, and of the existence of which he is but imperfectly aware. All of these mental possessions, however, are useful and valuable to him—even the lowest. The lowest may be used to advantage, under proper mastery, and are only dangerous to the man who allows them to master him instead of serving him as they should, considering his present stage of development.

In this consideration of the several mental planes we shall not confine ourselves to the technical occult terms given to these several planes, but will place them in general groups and describe the features and characteristics of each, rather than branch off into long explanations of the growth and reason of the several planes, which would take us far away from the practical consideration of the subject.

Beginning at the lowest point of the scale we see that man has a body. The body is composed of minute cells of protoplasm. These cells are built up of countless molecules, atoms and particles of matter—precisely the same matter that composes the rocks, trees, air, etc., around him. The Yogi philosophy tells us that even the atoms of matter have life and an elementary manifestation of mind, which causes them to group together according to the law of attraction, forming different elements, combinations, etc. This law of attraction is a mental operation, and is the first evidence of mental choice, action and response. Below this is Prana or Force, which, strictly speaking, is also a manifestation of mind, although for convenience we designate it as a separate manifestation of the Absolute.

And therefore we find that this law of attraction between the atoms and particles of matter is a mental action, and that it belongs to man's mental kingdom, because he has a body and this mental action is continually going on in his body.

So therefore this is the lowest mental plane to be considered in the makeup of the man. This plane is, of course, far sunken beneath the plane of consciousness, and is scarcely identified with the personality of the man at all, but rather belongs to the life of the whole, manifest in the rock as well as in the man.

But after these atoms have been grouped by the law of attraction and have formed molecules of matter, they are taken possession of by a higher mental activity and built up into cells by the mental action of the plant. The life impulse of the plant begins by drawing to it certain particles of inorganic matter—chemical elements—and then building them into a single cell. Oh, mystery of the cell! The intellect of man is unable to duplicate this wonderful process. The Mind Principle on the Vegetative Plane, however, knows exactly how to go to work to select and draw to itself just the elements needed to build up the single cell. Then taking up its abode in that cell—using it as a basis of operations, it proceeds to duplicate its previous performance, and so cell after cell is added, by the simple reproductive process of division and subdivision—the primitive and elemental sex process—until the mighty plant is built up. From the humblest vegetable organism up to the greatest oak the process is the same.

And it does not stop there. The body of man is also built up in just this way, and he has this vegetative mind also within him, below the plane of consciousness, of course. To many this thought of a vegetative mind may be somewhat startling. But let us remember that every part of our body has been built up from the vegetable cell. The unborn child starts with the coalition of two cells. These cells begin to build up the new body for the occupancy of the child—that is, the mind principle in the cells directs the work, of course—drawing upon the body of the mother for nourishment and supplies. The nourishment in the mother's blood, which supplies the material for the building up of the child's body, is obtained by the mother eating and assimilating the vegetable cells of plants, directly or indirectly. If she eats fruit, nuts, vegetables, etc., she obtains the nourishment of the plant life directly—if she eats meat she obtains it indirectly, for the animal from which the meat was taken built up the meat from vegetables. There is no two ways about this—all nourishment of the animal and human kingdom is obtained from the vegetable kingdom, directly or indirectly.

And the cell action in the child is identical with the cell action in the plant. Cells constantly reproducing themselves and building themselves up into bodily organs, parts, etc., under the direction and guidance of the mind principle. The child grows in this way until the hour of birth. It is born, and then the process is but slightly changed. The child begins to take nourishment either from the mother's milk or from the milk of the cow, or other forms of food. And as it grows larger it partakes of many different varieties of food. But always it obtains building material from the cell life of the plants.

And this great building up process is intelligent, purposeful, to a wonderful degree. Man with his boasted intellect cannot explain the real "thingness" of the process. A leading scientist who placed the egg of a small lizard under microscopical examination and then watched it slowly develop has said that it seemed as if some hand was tracing the outlines of the tiny vertebrae, and then building up around it. Think for a moment of the development of the germ within the egg of the hummingbird, or the ant, or the gnat, or the eagle. Every second a change may be noticed. The germ cell draws to itself nourishment from the other part of the egg, and then it grows and reproduces another cell. Then both cells divide—then subdivide until there are millions and millions and millions of cells. And all the while the building up process continues, and the bird or insect assumes shape and form, until at last the work is accomplished and the young bird emerges from the egg.

And the work thus commenced continues until the death of the animal. For there is a constant using-up and breaking-down of cell and tissue, which the organism must replace. And so the vegetative mind of the plant, or insect, or animal, or man, is constantly at work building up new cells from the food, throwing out worn-out and used-up material from the system. Not only this, but it attends to the circulation of the blood in order that the materials for the building up may be carried to all parts of the system. It attends to the digestion and assimilation of the food—the wonderful work of the organs of the body. It attends to the healing of wounds, the fight against disease, the care of the physical body. And all this out of the plane of consciousness—in the infant man the animal world, the vegetable kingdom—ever at work, untiring, intelligent, wonderful. And this plane of mind is in man as well as in the plant, and it does its work without aid from the conscious part of man, although man may interfere with it by adverse conscious thought, which seems to paralyze its efforts. Mental Healing is merely the restoring of normal conditions, so that this part of the body may do its work without the hindrance of adverse conscious thought.

On this plane of the mind is found all of the vital functions and operations. The work is done out-of-consciousness, and the consciousness is aware of this part of the mind only when it makes demands upon the conscious for food, etc. On this plane also resides the elementary instinct that tends toward reproduction and sexual activity. The demand of this part of the mind is always "increase and multiply," and according to the stage of growth of the individual is the mandate carried out, as we shall see presently. The elementary impulses and desires that we find rising into the field of consciousness come from this plane of the mind. Hunger, thirst and the reproductive desires are its messages to the higher parts of the mind. And these messages are natural and free from the abuses and prostitution often observed attached to them by the intellect of man in connection with his unrestrained animal impulses. Gluttony and unnatural lust arise not from the primitive demand of this plane of the mind—for the lower animals even are free from them to a great extent—but it is reserved for man to so prostitute these primitive natural tendencies, in order to gratify unnatural and artificial appetites, which serve to frustrate nature rather than to aid her.

As Life advanced in the scale and animal forms appeared on the scene new planes of mind were unfolded, in accordance to the necessity of the living forms. The animal was compelled to hunt for his food—to prey upon other forms, and to avoid being preyed upon by others. He was compelled to struggle for the unfoldment of latent powers of his mind that would give him means to play his part in the scheme of life. He was compelled to do certain things in order to live and reproduce his kind. And he demanded not in vain. For there came to him slowly an unfolding knowledge of the things necessary for the requirements of his life. We call this Instinct. But, pray remember, by Instinct we do not mean the still higher something that is really rudimentary Intellect that we notice in the higher animals. We are speaking now of the unreasoning instinct observed in the lower animals, and to a certain degree in man. This Instinctive plane of mentality causes the bird to build its nest before its eggs are laid, which instructs the animal mother how to care for its young when born, and after birth; which teaches the bee to construct its cell and to store up its honey. These and countless other things in animal life, and in the higher form of plant life, are manifestations of Instinct—that great plane of the mind. In fact, the greater part of the life of the animal is instinctive although the higher forms of animals have developed something like rudimentary Intellect or Reason, which enables them to meet new conditions where Intellect alone fails them.

And man has this plane of mind within him, below consciousness. In fact the lower forms of human life manifest but little Intellect, and live almost altogether according to their Instinctive impulses and desires.

Every man has this Instinctive mental region within him and from it are constantly arising impulses and desires to perplex and annoy him, as well as to serve him occasionally. The whole secret consists in whether the man has Mastery of his lower self or not.

From this plane of the mind arise the hereditary impulses coming down from generations of ancestors, reaching back to the cavemen, and still further back into the animal kingdom. A queer storehouse is this. Animal instincts—passions, appetites, desires, feelings, sensations, emotions, etc., are there. Hate, envy, jealousy, revenge, the lust of the animal seeking the gratification of his sexual impulses, etc., etc., are there, and are constantly intruding upon our attention until we have asserted our mastery. And often the failure to assert this mastery comes from an ignorance of the nature of the desire, etc. We have been taught that these thoughts were "bad" without being told *why*, and we have feared them and thought them the promptings of an impure nature, or a depraved mind, etc. This is all wrong. These things are not "bad" of themselves—they came to us honestly—they are our heritage from the past. They belong to the animal part of our nature, and were necessary to the animal in his stage of development. We have the whole menagerie within us, but that does not mean that we should turn the beasts loose upon ourselves or others. It was necessary for the animal to be fierce, full of fight, passionate, regardless of the rights of others, etc., but we have outgrown that stage of development, and it is ignoble for us to return to it, or to allow it to master us.

This lesson is not intended as a discourse upon Ethics or morals. We do not intend going into a discussion of the details of "Right and Wrong," for we have touched upon that phase of the subject in other works. But we feel justified in calling your attention to the fact that the human mind intuitively recognizes the "Rightness" of the living up to that which comes to us from the highest parts of the mind—the highest product of our unfoldment. And it likewise intuitively recognizes the "Wrongness" of the falling back into that which belongs to the lower stages of our mentality—to the animal part of us, that is our heritage from the past and that which has gone before.

While we may be puzzled about many details of morals and ethics and may not be able to "explain" why we consider certain things right or wrong, we still intuitively feel that the highest "Right" of which we are capable is the acting out of that which is coming to us from the highest pole of our mental being, and that the lowest "Wrong" consists in doing that which carries us back to the life of the lower animals, in so far as mentality is concerned. Not because there is anything absolutely "Wrong" in the mental processes and consequent of the animals in themselves—they are all right and perfectly natural in the animals—but we intuitively recognize that for us to fall back to the animal stage is a "going backward" in the scale of evolution. We intuitively shrink at an exhibition of brutality and animality on the part of a man or woman. We may not know just why, but a little reflection will show us that it is a sinking in the evolutionary scale, against which the spiritual part of us revolts and protests.

But this must not be construed to mean that the advanced soul looks upon the animal world with disgust or horror. On the contrary, there is nowhere to be found a higher respect for animal life and being than among the Yogi and other advanced souls. They delight in watching the animals filling their places in life—playing out their parts in the divine scheme of life. Their animal passions and desires are actions viewed sympathetically and lovingly by the advanced soul, and nothing "Wrong" or disgusting is seen there. And even the coarseness and brutality of the savage races are so regarded by these advanced souls. They see everything as natural according to the grade and degree of development of these people.

It is only when these advanced souls view the degeneracies of "civilized" life that they feel sorrow and pain. For here they see instances of devolution instead of evolution—degeneration instead of regeneration and advancement. And not only do they know this to be the fact, but the degenerate specimens of mankind themselves feel and know it. Compare the expression of the animal or savage going through their natural life actions and performances. See how free and natural are their expressions, how utterly apart are evidences of wrong doing. They have not as yet found out the fatal secret of Good and Evil—they have not as yet eaten the forbidden fruit. But, on the contrary, look into the faces of the degenerates and fallen souls of our civilized life. See the furtive glance and the self-consciousness of "Wrong" evident in every face. And this consciousness of "Wrong" bears heavily upon these people—it is heavier than the punishments heaped upon them. That nameless something called "conscience" may be smothered for a while, but sooner or later it comes to light and demands the pound of flesh from its victim.

And yet you will say that it seems hard to think that the same thing can be Right in one person and Wrong in another. This seems like a hard saying and a dangerous doctrine, but it is the Truth. And man instinctively recognizes it. He does not expect the same sense of moral responsibility in a young child, or in a savage, that he does in a mature, developed, civilized man. He may restrain the child and the savage, for self-protection and the welfare of all, but he realizes the distinction, or at least should do so. And not only is this true, but as man advances in the scale he casts off many ideas of "Wrong" that he once held, having outgrown the old ideas and having grown into new conceptions. And the tendency is always upward and onward. The tendency is constantly from Force and Restraint toward Love and Freedom. The ideal condition would be one in which there were no laws and no necessity for them—a condition in which men had ceased to do wrong because they had outgrown the desire rather than from fear or restraint or force. And while this condition as yet seems afar off, there is constantly going on an unfoldment of higher planes and faculties of the mind, which when once fully manifest in the race will work a complete revolution in ethics and laws and government—and for the better, of course. In the meantime Mankind moves along, doing the best it can, making a steady though slow progress.

There is another plane of the mind which is often called the "Instinct," but which is but a part of the plane of the Intellect, although its operations are largely below the field of consciousness. We allude to what may be called the "Habit Mind," in order to distinguish it from the Instinctive Plane. The difference is this: The Instinctive plane of mind is made up of the ordinary operations of the mind below the plane of the Intellect, and yet above the plane of the Vegetative mind—and also of the acquired experiences of the race, which have been transmitted by heredity, etc. But the "Habit Mind" contains only that which has been placed there by the person himself and which he has acquired by experience, habit, and observation, repeated so often until the mind knows it so well that it is carried below the field of consciousness and becomes "second nature," and akin to Instinct.

The textbooks upon psychology are filled with illustrations and examples of the habit phase or plane of the mental operations, and we do not think it necessary to repeat instances of the same kind here. Everyone is familiar with the fact that tasks which at first are learned only by considerable work and time soon become fixed in some part of the mind until their repetition calls for little or no exercise of conscious mental operation. In fact, some writers have claimed that no one really "learns" how to perform a task until he can perform it almost automatically. The pupil who in the early stages of piano playing finds it most difficult to control and manage his fingers, after a time is able to forget all about his fingering and devote his entire attention to the pages of his music, and after this he is able to apparently let his fingers play the entire piece of music by themselves without a thought on his part. The best performers have told us that in the moments of their highest efforts they are aware that the out-of-conscious portion of their mind is doing the work for them, and they are practically standing aside and witnessing the work being done. So true is this that in some cases it is related that if the performer's conscious mind attempts to take up the work the quality is impaired and the musician and the audience notice the difference.

The same thing is true in the case of the woman learning to operate the sewing machine. It is quite difficult at first, but gradually it grows to "run itself." Those who have mastered the typewriter have had the same experience. At first each letter had to be picked out with care and effort. After a gradual improvement the operator is enabled to devote her entire attention to the "copy" and let the fingers pick out the keys for themselves. Many operators learn rapid typewriting by so training the habit mind that it picks out the letter-keys by reason of their position, the letters being covered over in order to force the mind to adapt itself to the new requirements. A similar state of affairs exists wherever men or women have to use tools of any kind. The tool soon is recognized by the mind and used as if it were a part of the body, and no more conscious thought is devoted to the manipulation than we devote to the operation of walking, which, by the way, is learned by the child only by the expenditure of time and labor. It is astonishing how many things we do "automatically" in this way. Writers have called our attention to the fact that the average man cannot consciously inform you how he puts on his coat in the morning—which arm goes in first, how the coat is held, etc. But the habit mind knows—knows very well. Let the student stand up and put on his coat in the regular way, following the leadings of the habit mind. Then, after removing it, let him attempt to put it on by inserting the other arm first, for instance. He will be surprised to find out how awkward it will be for him, and how completely he has been depending upon the habit mind. And tomorrow morning let him find out which shoe the habit mind has been putting on him first and then try to reverse the order and notice how flurried and disturbed the habit mind will become, and how frantically it will signal to the conscious mind: "Something wrong up there!" Or try to button on your collar, reversing the order in which the tabs are placed over the button—right before left, or left before right, as the case may be, and notice the involuntary protest. Or, try to reverse the customary habit in walking and attempt to swing your right arm with the movement of your right leg, and so on, and you will find it will require the exercise of great willpower. Or, try to "change hands" and use your knife and fork. But we must stop giving examples and illustrations. Their number is countless.

Not only does the habit mind attend to physical actions, etc., but it also takes a hand in our mental operations. We soon acquire the habit of ceasing to consciously consider certain things, and the habit mind takes the matter for granted, and thereafter we will think automatically on those particular questions, unless we are shaken out of the habit by a rude jolt from the mind of someone else, or from the presentation of some conflicting idea occasioned by our own experience or reasoning processes. And the habit mind hates to be disturbed and compelled to revise its ideas. It fights against it, and rebels, and the result is that many of us are slaves to old outgrown ideas that we realize are false and untrue, but which we find that we "cannot exactly get rid of." In our future lessons we will give methods to get rid of these old outgrown ideas.

There are other planes of mind which have to do with the phenomena known as "psychic," by which is meant the phases of psychic phenomena known as clairvoyance, psychometry, telepathy, etc., but we shall not consider them in this lesson, for they belong to another part of the general subject. We have spoken of them in a general way in our *Fourteen Lessons in Yogi Philosophy*, etc.

And now we come to the plane of mind known to us as Intellect or the Reasoning Faculties. Webster defines the word Intellect as follows: The part or faculty of the human soul by which it knows, as distinguished from the power to feel and to will; the thinking faculty; the understanding. The same authority defines the word Reason as follows: "The faculty or capacity of the human mind by which it is distinguished from the intelligence of the inferior animals." We shall not attempt to go into a consideration of the conscious Intellect, for to do so we would be compelled to take up the space of the remaining lessons of the course, and besides, the student may find extended information on this subject in any of the textbooks on psychology. Instead we will consider other faculties and planes of mind which the said textbooks pass by rapidly, or perhaps deny. And one of these planes is that of Unconscious Reasoning, or Intellect. To many this term will seem paradoxical, but students of the unconscious will understand just what is meant.

Reasoning is not necessarily conscious in its operations, in fact, a greater part of the reasoning processes are performed below or above the conscious field. In our last lesson we have given a number of examples proving this fact, but a few more remarks may not be out of place, nor without interest to the student.

In our last lesson you will see many instances stated

in which the subconscious field of the Intellect worked out problems, and then after a time handed to the conscious reason the solution of the matter. This has occurred to many of us, if not indeed to all of us. Who has not endeavored to solve a problem or question of some sort and after "giving it up" has had it suddenly answered and flashed into consciousness when least expected. The experience is common to the race. While the majority of us have noticed these things, we have regarded them as exceptional and out of the general rule. Not so, however, with students of the mental planes. The latter have recognized these planes of reason, and have availed themselves of their knowledge by setting these unconscious faculties to work for them. In our next lesson we will give directions to our students regarding this accomplishment, which may prove of the greatest importance to those who will take the trouble to practice the directions given. It is a plan that is known to the majority of men who have "done things" in the world, the majority of them, however, having discovered the plan for themselves as the result of a need or demand upon the inner powers of mind.

The plane of mind immediately above that of Intellect is that known as Intuition. Intuition is defined by Webster as follows: "Direct apprehension or cognition; immediate knowledge, as in perception or consciousness, involving no reasoning process; quick or ready insight or apprehension." It is difficult to explain just what is meant by Intuition, except to those who have experienced it—and these people do not need the explanation. Intuition is just as real a mental faculty as is Intellect—or, to be more exact, is just as much a collection of mental faculties. Intuition is above the field of consciousness, and its messages are passed downward, though its processes are hidden. The race is gradually unfolding into the plane of Intuition, and the race will some day pass into full consciousness on that plane. In the meantime it gets but flashes and glimpses from the hidden region. Many of the best things we have come from that region. Art, music, the love of the beautiful and good poetry, the higher form of love, spiritual insight to a certain degree, intuitive perception of truth, etc., etc., come from this region. These things are not reasoned out by the intellect, but seem to spring full born from some unknown region of the mind.

In this wonderful region dwells Genius. Many, if not all of the great writers, poets, musicians, artists and other examples of genius have felt that their power came to them from some higher source. Many have thought that it emanated from some being kindly to them, who would inspire them with power and wisdom. Some transcendent power seemed to have been called into operation, and the worker would feel that his product or creation was not his handiwork, but that of some outside intelligence. The Greeks recognized this something in man, and called it man's "Daemon." Plutarch in his discourse on the daemon that guided Socrates speaks of the vision of Timarchus, who, in the case of Trophonius, saw spirits which were partly attached to human bodies, and partly over and above them, shining luminously over their heads. He was informed by the oracle that the part of the spirit which was immersed in the body was called the "soul," but that the outer and unimmersed portion was called the "daemon." The oracle also informed him that every man had his daemon, whom he is bound to obey; those who implicitly follow that guidance are the prophetic souls, the favorites of the gods. Goethe also spoke of the daemon as a power higher than the will, and which inspired certain natures with miraculous energy.

We may smile at these conceptions, but they are really very close to the truth. The higher regions of the mind, while belonging to the individual, and a part of himself, are so far above his ordinary consciousness that to all intents and purposes messages from them are as orders from another and higher soul. But still the voice is that of the "I," speaking through its sheaths as best it is able.

This power belongs to every one of us, although it manifests only in the degree that we are able to respond to it. It grows by faith and confidence, and closes itself up, and withdraws into its recesses when we doubt it and would question its veracity and reality. What we call "originality" comes from this region. The Intuitive faculties pass on to the conscious mind some perception of truth higher than the Intellect has been able to work out for itself, and lo! it is called the work of genius.

The advanced occultist knows that in the higher regions of the mind are locked up intuitive perceptions of all truth, and that he who can gain access to these regions will know everything intuitively, and as a matter of clear sight, without reasoning or explanation. The race has not as yet reached the heights of Intuition—it is just beginning to climb the foothills. But it is moving in the right direction. It will be well for us if we will open ourselves to the higher inner guidance, and be willing to be "led by the Spirit." This is a far different thing from being led by outside intelligence, which may, or may not, be qualified to lead. But the Spirit within each of us has our interests at heart and is desirous of our best good, and is not only ready but willing to take us by the hand and lead us on. The Higher Self is doing the best it can for our development and welfare, but is hampered by the confining sheaths. And alas, many of us glory in these sheaths and consider them the highest part of ourselves. Do not be afraid to let the light of the Spirit pierce through these confining sheaths and dissolve them. The Intuition, however, is not the Spirit, but is one of its channels of communication to us. There are other and still higher planes of mind, but the Intuition is the one next in the line of unfoldment, and we should open ourselves to its influence and welcome its unfoldment.

Above the plane of Intuition is that of the Cosmic Knowing, upon which we will find the consciousness of the Oneness of All. We have spoken of this plane in our lesson on the Unfoldment of Consciousness. When one is able to be "conscious" on this plane—this exalted plane of mind—he is able to see fully, plainly and completely that there is One Great Life underlying all the countless forms and shapes of manifestation. He is able to see that separateness is only "the working fiction of the Universe." He is able to see that each Ego is but a Centre of Consciousness in the great Ocean of Life—all in pursuance of the Divine Plan, and that he is moving forward toward higher and higher planes of manifestation, power and individuality, in order to take a greater and grander part in the Universal work and plans.

The Cosmic Knowing in its fullness has come to but few of the race, but many have had glimpses, more or less clear, of its transcendent wonder, and others are on the borderland of this plane. The race is unfolding gradually, slowly but surely, and those who have had this wonderful experience are preparing others for a like experience. The seed is being sown, and the harvest will come later. This and other phases of the higher forms of consciousness are before the race. The individuals who read this lesson are perhaps nearer to it than they think; their interest in the lessons is an indication of that hunger of the soul which is a prophecy of the satisfaction of the cry for spiritual bread. The Law of Life heeds these cries for aid and nourishment and responds accordingly, but along the lines of the highest wisdom and according to the *real requirements* of the individual.

Let us close this lesson with a quotation from *Light on the Path*, which bears directly upon the concluding thought. Read it carefully and let it sink down deep into your inner consciousness, and you will feel the thrill of joy that comes to him who is nearing the goal.

> Look for the flower to bloom in the silence that follows the storm; not till then.
>
> It shall grow, it will shoot up, it will make branches and leaves, and form buds while the storm lasts. But not until the entire personality of the man is dissolved and melted—not until it is held by the divine fragment which has created it, as a mere subject for grave experiment and experience—not until the whole nature has yielded and become subject unto its higher self, can the bloom open. Then will come a calm such as comes in a tropical country after the heavy rain, when nature works so swiftly that one may see her action. Such a calm will come to the harassed spirit. And in the deep silence the mysterious event will occur which will prove that the way has been found. Call it by whatever name you will. It is a voice that speaks where there is none to speak, it is a messenger that comes—a messenger without form or substance—or it is the flower of the soul that has opened. It cannot be described by any metaphor. But it can be felt after, looked for, and desired, even among the raging of the storm. The silence may last a moment of time, or it may last a thousand years. But it will end. Yet you will carry

its strength with you. Again and again the battle must be fought and won. It is only for an interval that nature can be still.

The concluding three lessons of this series will be devoted to a practical course of instruction in the development of the hidden planes of the mind, or rather, in the development of the power of the individual to master the same and make use of them in his life. He will be taught to master the lower principles, not only in the surmounting of them, but in the transmitting of the elemental forces toward his higher ends. Power may be obtained from this part of the mind, under the direction of the Will. And the student will be told how to set the unconscious Intellect to work for him. And he will be told how to develop and train the Will. We have now passed the line between the theoretical and the practical phases of the subject, and from now on it will be a case of train, develop, cultivate and apply. Knowing what lies back of it all, the student is now prepared to receive the instructions which he might have misused before.

Peace be with thee all.

NINTH LESSON—MANTRAM

I AM THE MASTER OF MY SOUL.

Subconsciousing

In the Ninth Lesson we called your attention to the fact that Reasoning was not necessarily conscious in its operations, and that, in fact, a large part of the rational processes of the mind are performed below or above the field of consciousness. And in the Eighth Lesson we gave you a number of examples illustrating this fact. We also gave you a number of cases in which the subconscious field of the Intellect worked out problems, and then after a time passed on to the conscious field of the Intellect the solution of the matter. In this lesson we purpose instructing you in the methods by which this part of the Intellect may be set to work for you. Many have stumbled upon bits of this truth for themselves, and, in fact, the majority of successful men and men who have attained eminence in any walk of life have made more or less use of this truth, although they seldom understand the reason of it.

Very few Western writers have recognized the work of this plane of the mind. They have given us full and ingenious theories and examples of the workings of the Instinctive Mind, and in some cases they have touched upon the workings and operations of the Intuitional planes, but in nearly every case they have treated the Intellect as something entirely confined to the Conscious plane of mentation. In this they have missed some of the most interesting and valuable manifestations of subconscious mentation.

In this lesson we will take up this particular phase of mentation, and trust to be able to point out the way to use it to the best advantage, giving some simple instructions that have been given by the Hindu teachers to their students for centuries past, such instructions of course, being modified by us to conform to the requirements and necessities of the Western student of today.

We have taken the liberty of bestowing a new title upon this phase of Mentation—we have thought it well to call it "Subconsciousing." The word "Sub," of course means "under; below"; and the word "Consciousing" is a favorite term employed by Prof. Elmer Gates, and means receiving impressions from the mind. In a general way, "Subconsciousing," as used in this lesson, may be understood to mean "using the subconscious mind, under orders of the conscious mind."

By referring to our Eighth Lesson, we see on page 183, mention made of the case of the man who indulged in "unconscious rumination," which happened to him when he read books presenting new points of view essentially opposed to his previous opinion. You will note that after days, weeks, or months, he found that to his great astonishment the old opinions were entirely rearranged, and new ones lodged there.

On the same page you will see mentioned the case of Sir William Hamilton, who discovered an important law of mathematics while walking with his wife. In this case he had been previously thinking of the missing link in his chain of reasoning, and the problem was worked out for him by the subconscious plane of his Intellect.

On the same page, and the one following, is found the case of Dr. Thompson, who gives an interesting account of the workings of this part of his mind, which caused him at times to experience a feeling of the uselessness of all voluntary effort, coupled with a feeling that the matter was working itself clear in his mind. He tells us that at times he seemed to be merely a passive instrument in the hands of some person other than himself, who compelled him to wait until the work was performed for him by some hidden region of the mind. When the subconscious part of the mind had completed its work, it would flash the message to his conscious mind, and he would begin to write.

On page 184 mention is also made of the great French chemist Berthelot, who relates that some of his best conceptions have flashed upon him as from the clear sky. In fact, the Eighth Lesson is largely made up of examples of this kind, and we ask the student to reread the same, in order to refresh his mind with the truth of the workings of the subconscious mentality.

But you will notice in nearly all the cases mentioned, that those who related instances of the help of the subconscious mind had merely stumbled upon the fact that there was a part of the mind below consciousness that could and would work out problems for one, if it could somehow be set in operation. And these people trusted to luck to start that part of the mind in operation. Or rather, they would saturate their conscious mind with a mass of material, like stuffing the stomach with food, and then bid the subconscious mind assort, separate, arrange and digest the mental food, just as does the stomach and digestive apparatus digest the natural food—outside of the realm of consciousness or volition. In none of the cases mentioned was the subconscious mind *directed* specially to perform its wonderful work. It was simply hoped that it might digest the mental material with which it had been stuffed—in pure self-defense. But there is a much better way, and we intend to tell you about it.

The Hindu Yogis, or rather those who instruct their pupils in Raja Yoga, give their students directions whereby they may *direct* their subconscious minds to perform mental tasks for them, just as one may direct another to perform a task. They teach them the methods whereby, after having accumulated the necessary materials, they may bid the subconscious mentality to sort it out, rearrange, analyze, and build up from it some bit of desired knowledge. More than this, they instruct their pupils to direct and order the subconscious mentality to search out and report to them certain information to be found only within the mind itself—some question of philosophy or metaphysics. And when such art has been acquired, the student or Yogi rests assured that the desired result will be forthcoming in due time, and consequently dismisses the matter from his conscious mind, and busies himself with other matters, knowing that day and night, incessantly, the subconsciousing process is going on, and that the subconscious mind is actively at work collecting the information, or working out the problem.

You will see at once the great superiority of this method over the old "hit-or-miss," "hope-it-will-work" plan pursued by those who have stumbled upon bits of the truth.

The Yogi teacher begins by impressing upon his students the fact that the mind is capable of extending outward toward an object, material or mental, and by examining it by methods inherent in itself, extracting knowledge regarding the object named. This is not a startling truth, because it is so common, everyone employing it more or less every day. But the process by which the knowledge is extracted is most wonderful, and really is performed below the plane of consciousness, the work of the conscious mind being chiefly concerned *in holding the Attention* upon the object. We have spoken of the importance of Attention in previous lessons, which it will be well for you to reread, at this time.

When the student is fully impressed with the details of the process of Attention, and the subsequent unfoldment of knowledge, the Yogi proceeds to inform him that there are other means of obtaining knowledge about an object, by the employment of which the Attention may be firmly directed toward the object and then afterwards held there *unconsciously*—that is, a portion of the Attention, or a subconscious phase of mentation, which will hold the subconscious mind firmly upon the work until accomplished, leaving the conscious Attention and mentality free to employ itself with other things.

The Yogis teach the students that this new form of Attention is far more intense and powerful than is the conscious Attention, for it cannot be disturbed or shaken, or distracted from its object, and that it will work away at its task for days, months, years, or a lifetime if necessary, according to the difficulty of the task, and in fact carries its work over from one life to another, unless recalled by the Will. They teach the student that in everyone's life there is going on a greater or lesser degree of this subconscious work, carried on in obedience to a strong desire for knowledge manifested in some former life, and bearing fruit only in the present existence. Many important discoveries have been made in obedience to this law. But it is not of this phase of the matter that we wish to speak in this lesson.

The Yogi theory is that the subconscious intellectual faculty may be set to work under the direction of orders given by the Will. All of you know how the subconscious mentality will take up an order of the Will, or a strong wish, that the person be awakened at a certain hour in order to catch a train. Or, in the same way how the remembrance of a certain engagement at, say, four o'clock, will flash into the mind when the hands of the clock approach the stated hour. Nearly everyone can recall instances of this sort in his own experience.

But the Yogis go much further than this. They claim that any and all faculties of the mind may be "set going," or working on any problem, if ordered thereto by the Will. In fact, the Yogis, and their advanced students have mastered this art to such a surprising extent that they find it unnecessary to do the drudgery of thinking in the conscious field, and prefer to relegate such mental work to the subconscious, reserving their conscious work for the consideration of digested information and thought presented to them by the subconscious mind.

Their directions to their students cover a great deal of ground, and extend over a long period of time, and many of the directions are quite complicated and full of detail. But we think that we can give our students an abbreviated and condensed idea in a few pages of the lesson. And the remaining lessons of the course will also throw additional light on the subject of subconscious mental action, in connection with other subjects.

The Yogi takes the student when the latter is much

bothered by a consideration of some knotty and perplexing philosophical subject. He bids the student relax every muscle—take the tension from every nerve—throw aside all mental strain, and then wait a few moments. Then the student is instructed to grasp the subject which he has had before his mind firmly and fixedly before his mental vision, by means of concentration. Then he is instructed to pass it on to the subconscious mentality by an effort of the Will, which effort is aided by forming a mental picture of the subject as a material substance, *or bundle of thought*, which is being bodily lifted up and dropped down a mental hatchway, or trapdoor, in which it sinks from sight. The student is then instructed to say to the subconscious mentality: "I wish this subject thoroughly analyzed, arranged, classified (and whatever else is desired) and then the results handed back to me. Attend to this."

The student is taught to speak to the subconscious mentality just as if it were a separate entity of being, which had been employed to do the work. He is also taught that *confident expectation* is an important part of the process, and that the degree of success depends upon the degree of this confident expectation.

In obstinate cases, the student is taught to use the Imagination freely, until he is able to make a mental image or picture of the subconscious mind doing what is required of it. This process clears away a mental path for the feet of the subconscious mind, which it will choose thereafter, as it prefers to follow the line of least resistance.

Of course much depends upon practice—practice makes perfect, you know, in everything else, and subconsciousing is no exception to the rule.

The student gradually acquires a proficiency in the art of

subconsciousing, and thereafter devotes his time to acquiring new facts for mental digestion, rather than bestowing it upon the mechanical act of thinking.

But a very important point to be remembered is that the Willpower back of the transferred thought-material, which Willpower is the cause of the subconscious action, depends very greatly upon the attention and interest given to the acquired material. This mass of thought-material which is to be digested, and threshed out by the subconscious mind, must be well saturated with interest and attention, in order to obtain the best results. In fact interest and attention are such important aids to the Will, that any consideration of the development and acquirement of Willpower is practically a development and acquirement of attention and interest. The student is referred to previous lessons in this course in which the importance of interest and attention is explained and described.

In acquiring the mass of thought-material which is to be passed on to the subconscious digestion, one must concentrate a great degree of interest and attention upon each item of thought-material gathered up. The gathering of this thought-material is a matter of the greatest importance, and must not be lightly passed by. One cannot hastily gather together all sorts of thought-material, and then expect the subconscious mind to do its work properly—it will not, in fact, and the student proceeding upon any such erroneous supposition is doomed to disappointment.

The proper way to proceed, is to take up each bit of thought-material in turn, and examine it with the greatest possible interest, and consequently the greatest attention, and then after having fairly saturated it with this interested attention, place it with the pile of material which, after a while, is to be passed on to the subconscious mentality. Then take up the next bit of material, and after giving it similar treatment, pass it along to the pile also. Then after a while when you have gathered up the main facts of the case, proceed to consider the mass as a whole, with interest and attention, giving it as it were a "general treatment." Then drop it down the trapdoor into the subconscious mind, with a strong command, "Attend to this thought-material," coupled with a strong expectant belief that your order will be obeyed.

The idea underlying this treatment of the thought-material with interest and attention is that by so doing a strong "Mental Image" is created, which may be easily handled by the subconscious mind. Remember that you are passing on "thoughts" for the subconsciousness to act upon, and that the more tangible and real these thoughts are, the better can they be handled. Therefore any plan that will build these thoughts up into "real" things is the plan to pursue. And attention and interest produce just this result.

If we may be pardoned for using a homely and commonplace illustration we would say that the idea may be grasped by the illustration of boiling an egg, whereby the fluid "white" and "yolk" becomes solid and real. Also the use of a shaving brush by a man, by which the thin lather is gradually worked up into a rich, thick, creamy mass, is an illustration. Again, the churning of butter is a favorite illustration of the Hindus, who thus call the attention of their students to the fact that thought-material if worked upon with attention and interest become "thought-forms" that may be handled by the mind just as the hands handle a material object. We ask you to think of these illustrations, for when you once grasp the idea that we wish to convey to you, you will have the secret of great thinking powers within your grasp.

And this power of subconsciousing is not confined alone to the consideration of philosophical questions. On the contrary it is applicable to every field of human thought, and may be properly employed in any and all of them. It is useful in solving the problems of everyday life and work, as well as to the higher flights of the human mind. And we wish every one of our students to realize that in this simple lesson we are giving them the key to a great mental power.

To realize just what we are offering to you, we would remind you of the old fairy tales of all races, in which there is to be found one or more tales telling of some poor cobbler, or tailor, or carpenter, as the case may be, who had by his good deeds, gained favor with the "brownies" or good fairies, who would come each night when the man and his family were asleep, and proceed to complete the work that the artisan had laid out for the morrow. The pieces of leather would be made into shoes; the cloth would be sewed into garments; the wood would be joined, and nailed together into boxes, chairs, benches and whatnot. But in each case the rough materials were prepared by the artisan himself during the day.

Well, that is just what we are trying to introduce to you. A clan of mental brownies, loving and kindly disposed toward you, who are anxious and willing to help you in your work. All you have to do is to give them the proper materials, and tell them what you want done, and they will do the rest. But these mental brownies are a part of your own mentality, remember, and no alien and foreign entities, as some have imagined.

A number of people who have accidentally discovered this power of the subconscious mind to work out problems, and to render other valuable service to its owner, have been led to suppose that the aid really came from some other entity or intelligence. Some have thought that the messages came from friends in the spirit land, and others have believed that some high intelligence—God or his angels—was working on their behalf. Without discussing spirit communication, or Divine messages, in both of which we believe (with certain provisional reservations) we feel justified in saying that the majority of cases of this kind may be referred to the subconscious workings of one's own mentality.

Each of us has "a friend" in our own mind—a score of them in fact, who delight in performing services for us, if we will but allow them to do so. Not only have we a Higher Self to whom we may turn for comfort and aid in times of deep distress and necessity, but we have these invisible mental workers on the subconscious plane, who are very willing and glad to perform much of our mental work for us, if we will but give them the material in proper shape.

It is very difficult to impart specific directions for obtaining these results, as each case must depend to a great extent upon the peculiar circumstances surrounding it. But we may say that the main thing needed is to "lick into shape" the material, and then pass it on to the subconscious mind in the manner spoken of a few moments ago. Let us run over a few cases wherein this principle may be applied.

Let us suppose that you are confronted with a problem consisting of an uncertainty as to which of two or more courses to adopt in some affair of life. Each course seems to have advantages and disadvantages, and you seem unable to pass upon the matter clearly and intelligently. The more you try the more perplexed and worried do you become. Your mind seems to tire of the matter, and manifests a state which may be called "mental nausea." This state will be apparent to anyone who has had much "thinking" to do. The average

person, however, persists in going over the matter, notwithstanding the tired condition of the mind, and its evident dis-
taste for a further consideration of the subject. They will keep
on forcing it back to the mind for consideration, and even at
nighttime will keep thrashing away at the subject. Now this
course is absurd. The mind recognizes that the work should
be done by another part of itself—its digestive region, in
fact—and naturally rebels at the finishing-up machinery being employed in work unsuited for it.

According to the Subconsciousing plan, the best thing
for the man to do would be for him first to calm and quiet his
mind. Then he should arrange the main features of the problem, together with the minor details in their proper places.
Then he should pass them slowly before him in review, giving a strong interest and attention to each fact and detail, as it
passes before him, *but without the slightest attempt to form a
decision, or come to a conclusion.* Then, having given the matter an interested and attentive review, let him *Will* that it pass
on to his subconscious mind, forming the mental image of
dropping it through the trapdoor, and at the same time giving the command of the Will, "Attend to this for me!"

Then dismiss the matter from your conscious mind, by
an effort of command of the Will. If you find it difficult to do
this, you may soon acquire the mastery by a frequent assertion, "I have dismissed this matter from my conscious mind,
and my subconscious mind will attend to it for me." Then,
endeavor to create a mental feeling of perfect trust and confidence in the matter, and avoid all worry or anxiety about it.
This may be somewhat difficult at the first trial, but will become a natural feeling after you have gained the confidence
arising from successful results in several cases. The matter
is one of practice, and, like anything else that is new, must

be acquired by perseverance and patience. It is well worth the time and trouble, and once acquired will be regarded as something in the nature of a treasure discovered in an unexpected place. The sense of tranquility and content—of calm and confidence—that comes to one who has practiced this plan, will of itself be worth all the trouble, not to speak of the main result. To one who has acquired this method, the old worries, frettings, and general "stewed up" feeling, will seem like a relic of barbarism. The new way opens up a world of new feelings and content.

In some cases the matter will be worked out by the subconscious mind in a very short time, and in fact we have known cases in which the answer would be flashed back almost instantly, almost like an inspiration. But in the majority of cases more or less time is required. The subconscious mind works very rapidly, but it takes time to arrange the thought-material properly, and to shape it into the desired forms. In the majority of cases it is well to let the matter rest until the next day—a fact that gives us a clue to the old advice to "sleep over" an important proposition, before passing a final decision.

If the matter does not present itself the following day, bring it up again before the conscious mind for review. You will find that it has shaped itself up considerably, and is assuming definite form and clearness. But right here—and this is important—do not make the mistake of again dissecting it, and meddling with it, and trying to arrange it with your conscious mind. But, instead, give it attention and interest in its new form, and then pass it back again to the subconscious mind for further work. You will find an improvement each time you examine it. But, right here another word of caution. Do not make the mistake of yielding to the impatience of the beginner, and keep on repeatedly bringing up the matter to see what is being done. Give it time to have the work done on it. Do not be like the boy who planted seeds, and who each day would pull them up to see whether they had sprouted, and how much.

Sooner or later, the subconscious mind will, of its own choice, lift up the matter and present it to you in its finished shape for the consideration of the conscious mind. The subconscious mind does not insist that you shall adopt its views, or accept its work, but merely hands out to you the result of its sorting, classifying and arranging. The choice and will still remain yours, but you will often find that there is seen to be one plan or path that stands out clearly from the others, and you will very likely adopt that one. The secret is that the subconscious mind with its wonderful patience and care has analyzed the matter, and has separated things before apparently connected. It has also found resemblances and has combined things heretofore considered opposed to each other. In short it has done for you all that you could have done with the expenditure of great work and time, and done it well. And then it lays the matter before you for your consideration and verdict.

Its whole work seems to have been in the nature of assorting, dissecting, analyzing, and arranging the evidence, and then presenting it before you in a clear, systematic shape. It does not attempt to exercise the judicial prerogative or function, but seems to recognize that its work ceases with the presentation of the edited evidence, and that of the conscious mind begins at the same point.

Now, do not confuse this work with that of the Intuition, which is a very different mental phase or plane. This subconscious working, just mentioned, plays an entirely different part. It is a good servant, and does not try to be more. The Intuition, on the contrary, is more like a higher friend—a friend at court, as it were, who gives us warnings and advice.

In our directions we have told you how to make use of this part of the mind, consciously and knowingly, so as to obtain the best results, and to get rid of worry and anxiety attendant upon unsettled questions. But, in fact, every one of us makes more or less use of this part of the mind unconsciously, and not realizing the important part it plays in our mental life. We are perplexed about a matter and keep it "on our minds" until we are forced to lay it aside by reason of some other demand, or when we sink to sleep. Often to our surprise we will find that when we next think of it the matter has somehow cleared up and straightened itself out, and we seem to have learned something about it that we did not know before. We do not understand it, and are apt to dismiss it as "just one of those things." In these lessons we are attempting to explain some of "those things," and to enable you to use them consciously and understandingly, instead of by chance, instinctively, and clumsily. We are teaching you Mastery of the Mind.

Now to apply the rule to another case. Suppose you wish to gather together all the information that you possess relating to a certain subject. In the first place it is certain that you know a very great deal more about any subject than you think you do. Stored away in the various recesses of the mind, or memory if you prefer that term, are stray bits of information and knowledge concerning almost any subject. But these bits of information are not associated with each other. You have never attempted to think attentively upon the particular question before you, and the facts are not correlated in the mind. It is just as if you had so many hundred pounds of anything scattered throughout the space of a large warehouse, a tiny bit here, and a tiny bit there, mixed up with thousands of other things.

You may prove this by sitting down sometime and letting your thoughts run along the line of some particular subject, and you will find emerging into the field of consciousness all sorts of information that you had apparently forgotten, and each fitting itself into its proper place. Every person has had experiences of this kind. But the work of gathering together the scattered scraps of knowledge is more or less tedious for the conscious mind, and the subconscious mind will do the work equally well with the wear and tear on the attention. In fact, it is the subconscious mind that *always* does the work, even when you think it is the conscious mind. All the conscious mind does is to hold the attention firmly upon the object before it, and then let the subconsciousness pass the material before it. But this holding the attention is tiresome work, and it is not necessary for it to expend its energies upon the details of the task, for the work may be done in an easier and simpler way.

The best way is to follow a plan similar to the one mentioned a few pages back. That is, to fix the interested attention firmly upon the question before you, until you manage to get a clear, vivid impression of *just what you want answered.* Then pass the whole matter into the subconscious mind with the command "Attend to this," and then leave it. Throw the whole matter off of your mind, and let the subconscious work go on. If possible let the matter run along until the next morning and then take it up for consideration, when, if you have proceeded properly you will find the matter worked out, arranged in logical sequence, so that your conscious attention will be able to clearly review the string of facts, examples, illustrations, experiences, etc., relating to the matter in question.

Now, many of you will say that you would like this plan to work in cases in which you have not the time to sleep over it. In such cases we will say that it is possible to cultivate a rapid method of subconsciousing, and in fact many businessmen and men of affairs have stumbled upon a similar plan, driven to the discovery by necessity. They will give a quick, comprehensive, strong flash of attention upon the subject, getting right to the heart of it, and then will let it rest in the subconscious mind for a moment or two, killing a minute or two of time in "preliminary conversation," until the first flash of answer comes to them. After the first flash, and taking hold of the first loose end of the subject that presents itself to them, they will unwind a string of information and "talk" about the subject that will surprise even themselves. Many lawyers have acquired this knowledge, and are what is known as "resourceful." Such men are often confronted with questions of conditions utterly unsuspected by them a moment before. Practice has taught them the folly of fear and loss of confidence at such moments, and has also impressed upon them the truth that something within them will come to the rescue. So, presenting a confident air, they will manage to say a few platitudes or commonplaces, while the subconscious mind is most rapidly gathering its materials for the answer. In a moment an opening thought "flashes upon" the man, and as he continues idea after idea passes before his conscious and eager attention, sometimes so rapidly that it is almost impossible to utter them and lo! the danger is over, and a brilliant success is often snatched from the jaws of an apparent failure and defeat. In such cases the mental demand upon the subconscious mind is not voiced in words, but is the result of a strong mental need. However, if one gives a quick verbal command *"Attend to this,"* the result will be heightened.

We have known of cases of men prominent in the world's affairs who made a practice of smoking a cigar during important business interviews, not because they particularly cared for tobacco, but because they had learned to appreciate the value of a moment's time for the mind to "gather itself together," as one man expressed it. A question would be asked, or a proposition advanced suddenly, demanding an immediate answer. Under the watchful eyes of the other party the questioned party tried not to show by his expression any indication of searching for an answer, for obvious reasons. So, instead, he would take a long puff at the cigar, then a slow attentive look at the ashes on its tip, and then another moment consumed in flicking the ash into the receptacle, and then came the answer, slowly, "Well, as to that-" or some other words of that kind, prefacing the real answer which had been rapidly framed by the subconscious mind in time to be uttered in its proper place. The few moments of time gained had been sufficient for the subconscious mind to gather up its materials, and the matter to be shaped properly, without any appearance of hesitation on the part of the answerer. All of this required practice, of course, but the principle may be seen through it all and in every similar case. The point is that the man, in such cases, sets some hidden part of his mind to work for him, and when he begins to speak the matter is at least roughly "licked into shape for him."

Our students will understand, of course, that this is not advice to smoke cigars during interviews of importance, but is merely given to illustrate the principle. We have known other men to twirl a lead pencil in their fingers in a lazy sort of fashion, and then drop it at the important moment. But we must cease giving examples of this kind, lest we be accused of giving instructions in worldly wisdom, instead of teaching the use of the mind. The impressive pause of the teacher, before answering his pupil's question, is also an example of the workings of this law. One often says "stop, let me think a moment," and during his pause he does not really consciously think at all, but stares ahead in a dreamy fashion, while his subconscious mind does the work for him, although he little suspects the nature of the operation. One has but to look around him to realize the importance and frequent application of this truth.

And not only may the subconscious mind be used in the directions indicated on preceding pages, but in nearly every perplexity and problem of life may it be called upon for help. These little subconscious brownies are ever at our disposal, and seem to be happy to be of service to us.

And so far from being apt to get us in a position of false dependence, it is calculated to make us self-confident—for we are calling upon a part of *ourselves*, not upon some outside intelligence. If those people who never feel satisfied unless they are getting "advice" from others would only cultivate the acquaintance of this little "home adviser" within them, they would lose that dependent attitude and frame of mind, and would grow self-confident and fearless. Just imagine the confidence of one who feels that he has within him a source of knowledge equal to that of the majority of those with whom he is likely to come in contact, and he feels less afraid to face them, and look them fearlessly in the eyes. He feels that his "mind" is not confined to the little field of consciousness, but is an area infinitely greater, containing a mass of information undreamed of. Everything that the man has inherited, or brought with him from past lives—everything that he has read, heard or seen, or experienced in this life, is hidden away there in some quarter of that great sub-conscious mind, and, if he will but give the command, the "essence" of all that knowledge is his. The details may not be presented to his consciousness (often it is not, for very good occult reasons) by the result, or essence of the knowledge will pass before his attention, with sufficient examples and illustrations, or arguments to enable him to make out "a good case" for himself.

In the next lesson we will call your attention to other features and qualities of this great field of mind, showing you how you can put it to work, and Master it. Remember, always, the "I" is the Master. And its Mastery must always be remembered and asserted over all phases and planes of the mind. Do not be a slave to the subconscious, but be its MASTER.

TENTH LESSON—MANTRAM

I have within me a great area of Mind that
is under my command, and subject to my
Mastery. This Mind is friendly to me, and is
glad to do my bidding, and obey my orders.
It will work for me when I ask it, and is
constant, untiring, and faithful. Knowing
this I am no longer afraid, ignorant or
uninformed. The "I" is master of it all, and
is asserting its authority. "I" am master
over Body, Mind, Consciousness, and
Subconsciousness. I am "I"—a Centre of
Power, Strength, and Knowledge. I am "I"—
and "I" am Spirit, a fragment from the
Divine Flame.

Subconscious Character Building

In our last lesson (the Tenth Lesson) we called your attention to the wonderful work of the subconscious regions of mentation in the direction of the performance of Intellectual work. Great as are the possibilities of this field of mentation in the direction named, they are equaled by the possibilities of building up character by similar methods.

Everyone realizes that one may change his character by a strenuous course of repression and training, and nearly all who read these lines have modified their characteristics somewhat by similar methods. But it is only of late years that the general public have become aware that Character might be modified, changed, and sometimes completely altered by means of an intelligent use of the subconscious faculties of the mind.

The word "Character" is derived from ancient terms meaning "to mark," "to engrave," etc., and some authorities inform us that the term originally arose from the word used by the Babylonian brickmakers to designate the trademark impressed by them upon their bricks, each maker having his own mark. This is interesting, in view of the recent theories regarding the cultivation of characteristics which may be found in the current Western works on psychology. But these theories are not new to the Yogi teachers of the East, who have employed similar methods for centuries past in training their students and pupils. The Yogis have long taught that a man's character was, practically, the crude character-stuff possessed by him at his birth, modified and shaped by outside influences in the case of the ordinary man, and by deliberate self-training and shaping by the wise man. Their pupils are examined regarding their characteristics, and then directed to repress the undesirable traits, and to cultivate the desirable ones.

The Yogi practice of Character Building is based upon the knowledge of the wonderful powers of the subconscious plane of the mind. The pupil is not required to pursue strenuous methods of repression or cultivation, but, on the contrary, is taught that such methods are opposed to nature's plans, and that the best way is to imitate nature and to gradually unfold the desired characteristics by means of focusing the willpower and attention upon them. The weeding out of undesirable characteristics is accomplished by the pupil cultivating the characteristics directly opposed to the undesirable ones. For instance, if the pupil desires to overcome Fear, he is not instructed to concentrate on Fear with the idea of killing it out, but, instead, is taught to mentally deny that he has Fear, and then to concentrate his attention upon the ideal of Courage. When Courage is developed, Fear is found to have faded away. The positive always overpowers the negative.

In the word "ideal" is found the secret of the Yogi method of subconscious character building. The teachings are to the effect that "ideals" may be built up by the bestowal of attention upon them. The student is given the example of a rose bush. He is taught that the plant will grow and flourish in the measure that care and attention is bestowed upon it and *vice versa*. He is taught that the ideal of some desired characteristic is a mental rosebush, and that by careful attention it will grow and put forth leaves and flowers. He is then given some minor mental trait to develop, and is taught to dwell upon it in thought—to exercise his imagination and to mentally "see" himself attaining the desired quality. He is given mantrams or affirmations to repeat, for the purpose of giving him a mental center around which to build an ideal. There is a mighty power in words, used in this way, providing that the user always thinks of the meaning of the words, and makes a mental picture of the quality expressed by them, instead of merely repeating them parrot fashion.

The Yogi student is trained gradually, until he acquires the power of conscious direction of the subconscious mind in the building up process, which power comes to anyone—Oriental or Occidental—who will take the trouble to practice. In fact, nearly everyone possesses and actively uses this power, although he may not be aware of it. One's character is largely the result of the quality of thoughts held in the mind, and of the mental pictures or ideals entertained by the person. The man who constantly sees and thinks of himself as unsuccessful and downtrodden is very apt to grow ideals of thought forms of these things until his whole nature is dominated by them, and his every act works toward the objectification of the thoughts. On the contrary, the man who makes an ideal of success and accomplishment finds that his whole mental nature seems to work toward that result—the objectification of the ideal. And so it is with every other ideal. The person who builds up a mental ideal of Jealousy will be very apt to objectify the same, and to unconsciously create condition that will give his Jealousy food upon which to feed. But this particular phase of the subject, properly belongs to our next lesson. This Eleventh Lesson is designed to point out the way by which people may mould their characters in any way they desire—supplanting undesirable characteristics by desirable ones, and developing desirable ideals into active characteristics. The mind is plastic to him who knows the secret of its manipulation.

The average person recognizes his strong and weak points of character, but is very apt to regard them as fixed and unalterable, or practically so. He thinks that he "is just as the Lord made him," and that is the end of it. He fails to recognize that his character is being unconsciously modified every day by association with others, whose suggestions are being absorbed and acted upon. And he fails to see that he is moulding his own character by taking interest in certain things, and allowing his mind to dwell upon them. He does not realize that he himself is really the maker of himself, from the raw and crude material given him at his birth. He makes himself negatively or positively. Negatively, if he allows himself to be moulded by the thoughts and ideals of others, and positively, if he moulds himself. Everyone is doing one or the other—perhaps both. The weak man is the one who allows himself to be made by others, and the strong man is the one who takes the building process in his own hands.

The process of Character-building is so delightfully simple that its importance is apt to be overlooked by the majority of persons who are made acquainted with it. It is only by actual practice and the experiencing of results that its wonderful possibilities are borne home to one.

The Yogi student is early taught the lesson of the power and importance of character building by some strong practical example. For instance, the student is found to have certain tastes of appetite, such as a like for certain things, and a corresponding dislike for others. The Yogi teacher instructs the student in the direction of cultivating a desire and taste for the disliked thing, and a dislike for the liked thing. He teaches the student to fix his mind on the two things, but in the direction of imagining that he likes the one thing and dislikes the other. The student is taught to make a mental picture of the desired conditions, and to say, for instance, "I loathe candy—I dislike even the sight of it," and, on the other hand, "I crave tart things—I revel in the taste of them," etc., etc., at the same time trying to reproduce the taste of sweet things accompanied with a loathing, and a taste of tart things, accompanied with a feeling of delight. After a bit the student finds that his tastes are actually changing in accordance with his thoughts, and in the end they have completely changed places. The truth of the theory is then borne home to the student, and he never forgets the lesson.

In order to reassure readers who might object to having the student left in this condition of reversed tastes, we may add that the Yogi teachers then teach him to get rid of the idea of the disliked thing, and teach him to cultivate a liking for all wholesome things, their theory being that the dislike of certain wholesome eatables has been caused by some suggestion in childhood, or by some prenatal impression, as wholesome eatables are made attractive to the taste by Nature. The idea of all this training, however, is not the cultivation of taste, but practice in mental training, and the bringing home to the student the truth of the fact that his nature is plastic to his Ego, and that it may be moulded at will, by concentration and intelligent practice. The reader of this lesson may experiment upon himself along the lines of the elementary Yogi practice as above mentioned, if he so desires. He will find it possible to entirely change his dislike for certain food, etc., by the methods mentioned above. He may likewise acquire a liking for heretofore distasteful tasks and duties, which he finds it necessary to perform.

The principle underlying the whole Yogi theory of Character Building by the subconscious Intellect, is that the Ego is Master of the mind, and that the mind is plastic to the commands of the Ego. The Ego or "I" of the individual is the one real, permanent, changeless principle of the individual, and the mind, like the body, is constantly changing, moving, growing, and dying. Just as the body may be developed and moulded by intelligent exercises, so may the mind be developed and shaped by the Ego if intelligent methods are followed.

The majority of people consider that Character is a fixed something, belonging to a man, that cannot be altered or changed. And yet they show by their everyday actions that at heart they do not believe this to be a fact, for they endeavor to change and mould the characters of those around them, by word of advice, counsel, praising or condemnation, etc.

It is not necessary to go into the matter of the consideration of the causes of character in this lesson. We will content ourselves by saying that these causes may be summed up, roughly, as follows: (1) Result of experiences in past lives; (2) Heredity; (3) Environment; (4) Suggestion from others; and (5) Auto-suggestion. But no matter how one's character has been formed, it may be modified, moulded, changed, and improved by the methods set forth in this lesson, which methods are similar to what is called by Western writers, "Auto-suggestion."

The underlying idea of Auto-suggestion is the "willing" of the individual that the changes take place in his mind, the willing being aided by intelligent and tried methods of creating the new ideal or thought-form. The first requisite for the changed condition must be "desire" for the change. Unless one really desires that the change take place, he is unable to bring his Will to bear on the task. There is a very close connection between Desire and Will. Will is not usually brought to bear upon anything unless it is inspired by Desire. Some people connect the word Desire with the lower inclinations, but it is equally applicable to the higher. If one fights off a low inclination or Desire, it is because he is possessed of a higher inclination or Desire. Many Desires are really compromises between two or more conflicting Desires—a sort of average Desire, as it were.

Unless one desires to change his character he will not make any move toward it. And in proportion to the strength of the desire, so will be the amount of willpower that is put in the task. The first thing for one to do in character building is to "want to do it." And if he finds that the "want" is not sufficiently strong to enable him to manifest the perseverance and effort necessary to bring it to a successful conclusion, then he should deliberately proceed to "build up the desire."

Desire may be built up by allowing the mind to dwell upon the subject until a desire is created. This rule works both ways, as many people have found out to their sorrow and misery. Not only may one build up a commendable desire in this way, but he may also build up a reprehensible one. A little thought will show you the truth of this statement. A young man has no desire to indulge in the excesses of a "fast" life. But after a while he hears, or reads something about others leading that sort of life, and he begins to allow his mind to dwell upon the subject, turning it around and examining it mentally, and going over it in his imagination. After a time he begins to find a desire gradually sending forth roots and branches, and if he continues to water the thing in his imagination, before long he will find within himself a blossoming inclination, which will try to insist upon expression in action. There is a great truth behind the words of the poet:

> Vice is a monster of so frightful mien,
> That to be hated needs but to be seen.
> Yet seen too oft, familiar with her face,
> We first endure, then pity, and then embrace.

And the follies and crimes of many a man have been due to the growing of desire within his mind, through this plan of planting the seed, and then carefully watering and tending to it—this cultivation of the growing desire. We have thought it well to give this word of warning because it will throw light upon many things that may have perplexed you, and because it may serve to call your attention to certain growing weeds of the mind that you have been nourishing.

But remember, always, that the force that leads downward may be transmuted and made to lead upward. It is just as easy to plant and grow wholesome desires as the other kind. If you are conscious of certain defects and deficiencies in your character (and who is not?) and yet find yourself not possessed of a strong enough desire to make the changes necessary, then you should commence by planting the desire seed and allowing it to grow by giving it constant care and attention. You should picture to yourself the advantages of acquiring the desirable traits of character of which you have thought. You should frequently go over and over them in your mind, imaging yourself in imagination as possessing them. You will then find that the growing desire will make headway and that you will gradually begin to "want to" possess that trait of character more and more. And when you begin to "want to" hard enough, you will find arising in your consciousness a feeling of the possession of sufficient Will-power to carry it through. Will follows the Desire. Cultivate a Desire and you will find back of it the Will to carry it through. Under the pressure of a very strong Desire men have accomplished feats akin to miracles.

If you find yourself in possession of desires that you feel are hurtful to you, you may rid yourself of them by deliberately starving them to death, and at the same time growing opposite desires. By refusing to think of the objectionable desires you refuse them the mental food upon which alone they can thrive. Just as you starve a plant by refusing it nourishing soil and water, so may you starve out an objectionable desire by refusing to give it mental food. *Remember this, for it is most important.* Refuse to allow the mind to dwell upon such desires, and resolutely turn aside the attention, *and, particularly, the imagination*, from the subject. This may call for the manifestation of a little willpower in the beginning, but it will become easier as you progress, and each victory will give you renewed strength for the next fight. But do not temporize with the desire—do not compromise with it—refuse to entertain the idea. In a fight of this kind each victory gives one added strength, and each defeat weakens one.

And while you are refusing to entertain the objectionable guest you must be sure to grow a desire of an entirely opposite nature—a desire directly opposed to the one you are starving to death. Picture the opposite desire, and think of it often. Let your mind dwell upon it lovingly and let the imagination help to build it up into form. Think of the advantages that will arise to you when you fully possess it, and let the imagination picture you as in full possession of it, and acting out your new part in life strong and vigorous in your newfound power.

All this will gradually lead you to the point where you will "want to" possess this power. Then you must be ready for the next step which is "Faith" or "Confident Expectation."

Now, faith or confident expectation is not made to order in most persons, and in such cases one must acquire it gradually. Many of you who read these lines will have an understanding of the subject that will give you this faith. But to those who lack it, we suggest that they practice on some trivial phases of the mental makeup, some petty trait of character, in which the victory will be easy and simple. From this stage they should work up to more difficult tasks, until at last they gain that faith or confident expectation that comes from persevering practice.

The greater the degree of faith or confident expectation that one carries with him in this task of character building, the greater will be his success. And this because of well-established psychological laws. Faith or confident expectation clears away the mental path and renders the work easier, while doubt or lack of faith retards the work, and acts as obstacles and stumbling blocks. Strong Desire, and Faith, or confident expectation are the first two steps. The third is Willpower.

By Willpower we do not mean that strenuous, clenching-of-fist-and-frowning-brow thing that many think of when they say "Will." Will is not manifested in this way. The true Will is called into play by one realizing the "I" part of himself and speaking the word of command from that center of power and strength. It is the voice of the "I." And it is needed in this work of character building.

So now you are ready for work, being possessed of (1) Strong Desire; (2) Faith or Confident Expectation; and (3) Willpower. With such a triple-weapon nothing but Success is possible.

Then comes the actual work. The first thing to do is to lay the track for a new Character Habit. "Habit?" you may ask in surprise. Yes, Habit! For that word gives the secret of the whole thing. Our characters are made up of inherited or acquired habits. Think over this a little and you will see the truth of it. You do certain things without a thought, because you have gotten into the habit of doing them. You act in certain ways because you have established the habit. You are in the habit of being truthful, honest, virtuous, because you have established the habit of being so. Do you doubt this? Then look around you—or look within your own heart, and you will see that you have lost some of your old habits of action, and have acquired new ones. The building up of Character is the building up of Habits. And the changing of Character is the changing of Habits. It will be well for you to settle this fact in your own mind, for it will give you the secret of many things connected with the subject.

And, remember this, that Habit is almost entirely a matter of the subconscious mentality. It is true that Habits originate in the conscious mind, but as they are established they sink down into the depths of the subconscious mentality, and thereafter become "second nature," which, by the way, is often more powerful than the original nature of the person. The Duke of Wellington said that habit was as strong as ten natures, and he proceeded to drill habits into his army until they found it natural to act in accordance with the habits pounded into them during the drills. Darwin relates an interesting instance of the force of habit over the reason. He found that his habit of starting back at the sudden approach of danger was so firmly established that no willpower could enable him to keep his face pressed up against the cage of the cobra in the Zoological Gardens when the snake struck at him, although he knew the glass was so thick that there could be no danger, and although he exerted the full force of his will. But we venture to say that one could overcome even this strongly ingrained habit, by gradually training the subconscious mentality and establishing a new habit of thought and action.

It is not only during the actual process of "willing" the new habit that the work of making the new mental path goes on. In fact, the Yogis believe that the principal part of the work goes on subconsciously between the intervals of command, and that the real progress is made in that way, just as the real work of solving the problem is performed subconsciously, as related in our last lesson. As an example, we may call your attention to some instances of the cultivation of physical habits. A physical task learned in the evening is much easier to perform the following morning than it was the night before, and still easier the following Monday morning than it was on the Saturday afternoon previous. The Germans have a saying that "we learn to skate in summer, and to swim in winter," meaning that the impression passed on to the subconscious mentality deepens and broadens during the interval of rest. The best plan is to make frequent, sharp impressions, and then to allow reasonable periods of rest in order to give the subconscious mentality the opportunity to do its work. By "sharp" impressions we mean impressions given under *strong attention*, as we have mentioned in some of the earlier lessons of this series.

A writer has well said: "Sow an act, reap a habit; sow a habit, reap a character; sow a character, reap a destiny," thus recognizing habit as the source of character. We recognize this truth in our training of children, forming goods habits of character by constant repetition, by watchfulness, etc. Habit acts as a *motive* when established, so that while we think we are acting without motive we may be acting under the strong motive power of some well-established habit. Herbert Spencer has well said: "The habitually honest man does what is right, not consciously because he 'ought' but with simple satisfaction; and is ill at ease till it is done." Some may object that this idea of Habit as a basis of Character may do away with the idea of a developed moral conscientiousness, as for instance, Josiah Royce who says: "The establishment of organized habit is never in itself enough to ensure the growth of an enlightened moral conscientiousness" but to such we would say that one must "want to" cultivate a high character before he will create the habits usual to the same, and the "want to" is the sign of the "moral conscientiousness," rather than the habit. And the same is true of the "ought to" side of the subject. The "ought to" arises in the conscious mind in the beginning, and inspires the cultivation of the habit, although the latter after a while becomes automatic, a matter of the subconscious mentality, without any "ought to" attachment. It then becomes a matter of "like to."

Thus we see that the moulding, modifying, changing, and building of Character is largely a matter of the establishing of Habits. And what is the best way to establish Habits? becomes our next question. The answer of the Yogi is: "Establish a Mental Image, and then build your Habit around it." And in that sentence he has condensed a whole system.

Everything we see having a form is built around a mental image—either the mental image of some man, some animal, or of the Absolute. This is the rule of the universe, and in the matter of character-building we but follow a well-established rule. When we wish to build a house, we first think of "house" in a general way. Then we begin to think of "what kind" of a house. Then we go into details. Then we consult an architect, and he makes us a plan, which plan is his mental image, suggested by our mental image. Then, the plan once decided upon, we consult the builder, and at last the house stands completed—an objectified Mental Image. And so it is with every created thing—all manifestations of a Mental Image.

And so, when we wish to establish a trait of Character, we must form a clear, distinct Mental Image of what we wish to be. This is an important step. Make your picture clear and distinct, and fasten it in your mind. Then begin to build around it. Let your thoughts dwell upon the mental picture. Let your imagination see yourself as possessed of the desired trait, and *acting it out*. Act it out in your imagination, over and over again, as often as possible, persevering, and continuously, seeing yourself manifesting the trait under a variety of circumstances and conditions. As you continue to do this you will find that you will gradually begin to express the thought in action—to objectify the subjective mental image. It will become "natural" for you to act more and more in accordance with your mental image, until at last the new habit will become firmly fixed in your mind, and will become your natural mode of action and expression.

This is no vague, visionary theory. It is a well-known and proven psychological fact, and thousands have worked marvelous changes in their character by its means.

Not only may one elevate his moral character in this

way, but he may mould his "work-a-day" self to better conform to the needs of his environment and occupation. If one
lacks Perseverance, he may attain it; if one is filled with Fear,
he may supplant it with Fearlessness; if one lacks Self-confidence, he may gain it. In fact, there is no trait that may not be
developed in this way. People have literally "made themselves
over" by following this method of character-building. The
great trouble with the race has been that persons have not
realized that they *could* do these things. They have thought
that they were doomed to remain just the creatures that they
found themselves to be. They did not realize that the work
of creation was not ended, and that they had within themselves a creative power adapted to the needs of their case.
When man first realizes this truth, and proves it by practice,
he becomes another being. He finds himself superior to environment, and training—he finds that he may ride over these
things. He makes *his own environment*, and *he trains himself*.

In some of the larger schools in England and the Unit-
ed States, certain scholars who have developed and manifested the ability to control themselves and their actions are
placed on the roll of a grade called the "Self-governed grade."
Those in this grade act as if they had memorized the following words of Herbert Spencer: "In the supremacy of self-con-
trol consists one of the perfections of the ideal man. Not to
be impulsive—not to be spurred hither and thither by each
desire—but to be self-restrained, self-balanced, governed by
the just decision of the feelings in council assembled ... that
it is which moral education strives to produce." And this is
the desire of the writer of this lesson—to place each student
in the "Self-governed class."

We cannot attempt, in the short space of a single lesson, to map out a course of instruction in Character Building

adapted to the special needs of each individual. But we think that what we have said on the subject should be sufficient to point out the method for each student to map out a course for himself, following the general rules given above. As a help to the student, however, we will give a brief course of instruction for the cultivation of one desirable trait of character. The general plan of this course may be adapted to fit the requirements of *any other case*, if intelligence is used by the student. The case we have selected is that of a student who has been suffering from "a lack of Moral Courage—a lack of Self-Confidence—an inability to maintain my poise in the presence of other people—an inability to say 'No!'—a feeling of Inferiority to those with whom I come in contact." The brief outline of the course of practice given in this case is herewith given:

PRELIMINARY THOUGHT. You should fix firmly in your mind the fact that you are the Equal of any and every man. You come from the same source. You are an expression of the same One Life. In the eyes of the Absolute you are the equal of any man, even the highest in the land. Truth is "Things as God sees them"—and in Truth you and the man are equal, and, at the last, One. All feelings of Inferiority are illusions, errors, and lies, and have no existence in Truth. When in the company of others remember this fact and realize that the Life Principle in you is talking to the Life Principle in them. Let the Life Principle flow through you, and endeavor to forget your personal self. At the same time, endeavor to see that same Life Principle, behind and beyond the personality of the person in whose presence you are. He is by a personality hiding the Life Principle, just as you are. Nothing more—nothing less! You are both One in Truth. Let the conscious of the "I" beam forth and you will experience an uplift and sense of Courage, and the other will likewise feel it. You have within you the Source of Courage, Moral and Physical, and you have naught to Fear—Fearlessness is your Divine Heritage, avail yourself of it. You have Self-Conscience, for the Self is the "I" within you, not the petty personality, and you must have confidence in that "I." Retreat within yourself until you feel the presence of the "I," and then will you have a Self-Confidence that nothing can shake or disturb. Once having attained the permanent consciousness of the "I," you will have poise. Once having realized that you are a Center of Power, you will have no difficulty in saying "No!" when it is right to do so. Once having realized your true nature—your Real Self—you will lose all sense of Inferiority, and will know that you are a manifestation of the One Life and have behind you the strength, power, and grandeur of the Cosmos. Begin by realizing YOURSELF, and then proceed with the following methods of training the mind.

WORD IMAGES. It is difficult for the mind to build itself around an idea, unless that idea be expressed in words. A word is the center of an idea, just as the idea is the center of the mental image, and the mental image the center of the growing mental habit. Therefore, the Yogis always lay great stress upon the use of words in this way. In the particular case before us, we should suggest the holding before you of a few words crystallizing the main thought. We suggest the words "I Am"; Courage; Confidence; Poise; Firmness; Equality. Commit these words to memory, and then endeavor to fix in your mind a clear conception of the meaning of each word, so that each may stand for a Live Idea when you say it. Beware of parrotlike or phonographic repetition. Let each word's meaning stand out clearly before you, so that when you repeat it you may *feel* its meaning. Repeat the words over frequently, when opportunity presents itself, and you will soon begin to notice that they act as a strong mental tonic upon you, producing a bracing, energizing effect. And each time you repeat the words, understandingly, you have done something to clear away the mental path over which you wish to travel.

PRACTICE. When you are at leisure, and are able to indulge in "daydreams" without injury to your affairs of life, call your imagination into play and endeavor to picture yourself as being possessed of the qualities indicated by the words named. Picture yourself under the most trying circumstances, making use of the desired qualities, and manifesting them fully. Endeavor to picture yourself as acting out your part well, and exhibiting the desired qualities. Do not be ashamed to indulge in these daydreams, for they are the prophecies of the things to follow, and you are but rehearsing your part before the day of the performance. Practice makes perfect, and if you accustom yourself to acting in a certain way in imagination, you will find it much easier to play your part when the real performance occurs. This may seem childish to many of you, but if you have an actor among your acquaintances, consult him about it, and you will find that he will heartily recommend it. He will tell you what practice does for one in this direction, and how repeated practice and rehearsals may fix a character so firmly in a man's mind that he may find it difficult to divest himself of it after a time. Choose well the part you wish to play—the character you wish to be yours—and then after fixing it well in your mind, practice, practice, practice. Keep your ideal constantly before you, and endeavor to grow into it. And you will succeed, if you exercise patience and perseverance.

But, more than this. Do not confine your practice to mere private rehearsal. You need some "dress rehearsals" as well—rehearsals in public. Therefore, after you get well started in your work, manage to exercise your growing character-habits in your everyday life. Pick out the little cases first and "try it on them." You will find that you will be able to overcome conditions that formerly bothered you much. You will become conscious of a growing strength and power coming from within, and you will recognize that you are indeed a changed person. Let your thought express itself in action, whenever you get a good chance. But do not try to force chances just to try your strength. Do not, for instance, try to force people to ask for favors that you may say "No!" You will find plenty of genuine tests without forcing any. Accustom yourself to looking people in the eye, and feeling the power that is back of you, and within you. You will soon be able to see through their personality, and realize that it is just one portion of the One Life gazing at another portion, and that therefore there is nothing to be afraid of. A realization of your Real Self will enable you to maintain your poise under trying circumstances, if you will but throw aside your false idea about your personality. Forget yourself—your little personal self—for a while, and fix your mind on the Universal Self of which you are a part. All these things that have worried you are but incidents of the Personal Life, and are seen to be illusions when viewed from the standpoint of the Universal Life.

Carry the Universal Life with you as much as possible into your everyday life. It belongs there as much as anywhere, and will prove to be a tower of strength and refuge to you in the perplexing situations of your busy life.

Remember always that the Ego is master of the mental

states and habits, and that the Will is the direct instrument of the Ego, and is always ready for its use. Let your soul be filled with the strong Desire to cultivate those mental habits that will make you Strong. Nature's plan is to produce Strong Individual expressions of herself, and she will be glad to give you her aid in becoming strong. The man who wishes to strengthen himself will always find great forces back of him to aid him in the work, for is he not carrying out one of Nature's pet plans, and one which she has been striving for throughout the ages. Anything that tends to make you realize and express your Mastery, tends to strengthen you, and places at your disposal Nature's aid. You may witness this in everyday life—Nature seems to like *strong* individuals, and delights in pushing them ahead. By Mastery, we mean mastery over your own lower nature, as well as over outside nature, of course. The "I" is Master—forget it not, O student, and assert it constantly. Peace be with you.

ELEVENTH LESSON—MANTRAM

I am the Master of my Mental Habits—I control
my Character. I Will to be Strong, and summon
the forces of my Nature to my aid.

Subconscious Influences

In this lesson we wish to touch upon a certain feature of sub-conscious mentation that has been much dwelt upon by certain schools of western writers and students during the past twenty years, but which has also been misunderstood, and, alas, too often misused, by some of those who have been at-tracted to the subject. We allude to what has been called the "Power of Thought." While this power is very real, and like any other of the forces of nature may be properly used and applied in our everyday life, still many students of the pow-er of the Mind have misused it and have stooped to practic-es worthy only of the followers of the schools of "Black Mag-ic." We hear on all sides of the use of "treatments" for selfish and often base ends, those following these practices seeming to be in utter ignorance of the occult laws brought into oper-ation, and the terrible reaction inevitably falling to the lot of those practicing this negative form of mental influence. We have been amazed at the prevailing ignorance concerning the nature and effects of this improper use of mental force, and at the same time, at the common custom of such selfish, improper uses. This, more particularly, when the true occultist knows that these things are not necessary, even to those who seek "Success" by mental forces. There is a true method of the use of mental forces, as well as an improper use, and we trust that in this lesson we may be able to bring the matter sharply and clearly before the minds of our students.

In our first course (The *Fourteen Lessons*) in the several lessons entitled, respectively, "Thought Dynamics," "Telepathy, etc.," and "Psychic Influence," we have given a general idea of the effect of one mind upon other minds, and many other writers have called the attention of the Western world to the same facts. There has been a general awakening of interest in this phase of the subject among the Western people of late years, and many and wonderful are the theories that have been advanced among the conflicting schools regarding the matter. But, notwithstanding the conflicting theories, there is a general agreement upon the fundamental facts. They all agree that the mental forces may be used to affect oneself and others, and many have started in to use these mental forces for their own selfish ends and purposes, believing that they were fully justified in so doing, and being unaware of the web of psychic causes and effects which they were weaving around them by their practices.

Now, at the beginning, let us impress upon the minds of our students the fact that while it is undoubtedly true that people who are unaware of the true sources of strength within them, may be, and often are affected by mental force exerted by others, it is equally true that no one can be adversely affected in this way providing he realizes the "I" within himself, which is the only Real part of him, and which is an impregnable tower of strength against the assaults of others.

There is no cause for all of this fear that is being manifested by many Western students of thought-power, who are in constant dread of being "treated" adversely by other people. The man or woman who realizes the "I" within, may by the slightest exercise of the Will surround himself with a mental aura which will repel adverse thought-waves emanating from the minds of others. Nay, more than this—the habitual recognition of the "I," and a few moments' meditation upon it each day, will of itself erect such an aura, and will charge this aura with a vitality that will turn back adverse thought, and cause it to return to the source from which it came, where it will serve the good purpose of bringing to the mistaken mind originating it, the conviction that such practices are hurtful and to be avoided.

This realization of the "I," which we brought out in the first few lessons of the present series, is the best and only real method of self-protection. This may be easily understood, when we remind you that the whole phenomena of mental influencing belongs to the "illusion" side of existence—the negative side—and that the Real and Positive side must of necessity be stronger. Nothing can affect the Real in you—and the nearer you get to the Real, in realization and understanding, the stronger do you become. *This is the whole secret*. Think it over.

But, there are comparatively few people who are able to rest firmly in the "I" consciousness all the time and the others demand help while they are growing. To such, we would say "Creep as close the Realization of the I as possible, and rest your spiritual feet firmly upon the rock of the Real Self." If you feel that people, circumstances, or things are influencing you unduly, stand up boldly, and deny the influence. Say something like this, "I DENY the power or influence of persons, circumstances, or things to adversely affect me. I ASSERT my Reality, Power and Dominion over these things." These words may seem very simple, but when uttered with the consciousness of the Truth underlying them, they become as a mighty force. You will understand, of course, that there is no magic or virtue in the words themselves—that is, in the grouping of the letters forming the words, or the sounds of the words—the virtue resting in the *idea* of which the words are the expression. You will be surprised at the effect of this STATEMENT upon depressing, or adverse influences surrounding you. If you—*you* who are reading these words now—feel yourself subject to any adverse or depressing influences, will then stand up erect, throwing your shoulders back, raising your head, and looking boldly and fearlessly ahead, and repeat these words firmly, and with faith, you will feel the adverse influences disappearing. You will almost see the clouds falling back from you. Try it now, before reading further, and you will become conscious of a new strength and power.

You are perfectly justified in thus denying adverse influence. You have a perfect right to drive back threatening or depressing thought-clouds. You have a perfect right to take your stand upon the Rock of Truth—your Real Self—and demand your Freedom. These negative thoughts of the world in general, and of some people in particular, belong to the dark side of life, and you have a right to demand freedom from them. You do not belong to the same idea of life, and it is your privilege—yes, your duty—to repel them and bid them disappear from your horizon. You are a Child of Light, and it is your right and duty to assert your freedom from the things of darkness. You are merely asserting the Truth when you affirm your superiority and dominion over these dark forces.

And in the measure of your Recognition and Faith, will be the power at your disposal. Faith and Recognition renders man a god. If we could but fully recognize and realize just what we are, we could rise above this entire plane of negative, dark world of thought. But we have become so blinded and stupefied with the race-thought of fear and weakness, and so hypnotized with the suggestions of weakness that we hear on all sides of us, that even the best of us find it hard to avoid occasionally sinking back into the lower depths of despair and discouragement. But, let us remember this, brothers and sisters, that these periods of "backsliding" become less frequent, and last a shorter time, as we proceed. By and by we shall escape them altogether.

Some may think that we are laying too much stress upon the negative side of the question, but we feel that what we have said is timely, and much needed by many who read these lessons. There has been so much said regarding this negative, adverse power of thought, that it is well that all should be taught that it is in their power to rise above this thing—that the weapon for its defeat is already in their hand.

The most advanced student may occasionally forget that he is superior to the adverse influence of the race-thought, and other clouds of thought influence that happen to be in his neighborhood. When we think of how few there are who are sending forth the positive, hopeful, thought-waves, and how many are sending forth continually the thoughts of discouragement, fear, and despair, it is no wonder that at times there comes to us a feeling of discouragement, helplessness, and "what's the use." But we must be ever alert, to stand up and *deny these things out of existence* so far as our personal thought world is concerned. There is a wonderful occult truth in the last sentence. We are the makers, preservers, and destroyers of our personal thought-world. We may bring into it that which we desire to appear; we may keep there what we wish, cultivating, developing and unfolding the thought-forms that we desire; we may destroy that which we wish to keep out. The "I" is the master of its thought-world. Think over this great truth, O student! By Desire we call into existence—by affirmation we preserve and encourage—by Denial we destroy. The Hindus in their popular religious conceptions picture the One Being as a Trinity, composed of Brahma, the Creator; Vishnu, the Preserver, and Shiva, the Destroyer—not three gods, as is commonly supposed, but a Trinity composed of three aspects of Deity or Being. This idea of the threefold Being is also applicable to the Individual—"as above so below." The "I" is the Being of the Individual, and the thought-world is its manifestation. It creates, preserves, and destroys—as it Will. Carry this idea with you, and realize that your individual thought-world is your own field of manifestation. In it you are constantly creating—constantly preserving—constantly destroying. And if you can destroy anything in your own thought-world you remove it from its field of activity, so far as you are concerned. And if you create anything in your own thought-world, you bring it into active being, so far as you are concerned. And if you preserve anything, you keep it by you in effect and full operation and influence in your life. This truth belongs to the higher phases of the subject, for its explanation is inextricably bound up in the explanation of the "Thing-in-Itself"—the Absolute and Its Manifestations. But even what we have said above, should give to the alert student sufficient notice to cause him to grasp the facts of the case, and to apply the principles in his own life.

If one lives on the plane of the race-thought, he is sub-

ject to its laws, for the law of cause and effect is in full operation on each plane of life. But when one raises himself above
the race-thought, and on to the plane of the Recognition of
the Real Self—The "I"—then does he extricate himself from
the lower laws of cause and effect, and places himself on a
higher plane of causation, in which he plays a much higher
part. And so we are constantly reminding you that your tower of strength and refuge lies on the higher plane. But, nevertheless, we must deal with the things and laws of the lower plane, because very few who read these lessons are able
to rest entirely upon the higher plane. The great majority of
them have done no more than to lift themselves partially on
to the higher plane, and they are consequently living on both
planes, partly in each, the consequence being that there is a
struggle between the conflicting laws of the two planes. The
present stage is one of the hardest on the Path of Attainment,
and resembles the birth-pains of the physical body. But you
are being born into a higher plane, and the pain after becoming the most acute will begin to ease, and in the end will disappear, and then will come peace and calm. When the pain
becomes the most acute, then be cheered with the certainty
that you have reached the crisis of your new spiritual birth,
and that you will soon gain peace. And then you will see that
the peace and bliss will be worth all the pain and struggle.
Be brave, fellow followers of The Path—Deliverance is nigh.
Soon will come the Silence that follows the Storm. The pain
that you are experiencing—ah, well do we know that you are
experiencing the pain—is not punishment, but is a necessary
part of your growth. All Life follows this plan—the pains of
labor and birth ever precede the Deliverance. Such is Life—
and Life is based upon Truth—and all is well with the world.
We did not intend to speak of these things in this lesson, but

as we write there comes to us a great cry for help and a word of encouragement and hope, from the Class which is taking this course of lessons, and we feel bound to respond as we have done. Peace be with you—one and all.

And, now we will begin our consideration of the laws governing what we have called "Subconscious Influence."

All students of the Occult are aware of the fact that men may be, and are, largely influenced by the thoughts of others. Not only is this the case in instances where thoughts are directed from the mind of one person to the mind of another, but also when there is no special direction or intention in the thought sent forth. The vibrations of thoughts linger in the astral atmosphere long after the effort that sent forth the thought has passed. The astral atmosphere is charged with the vibrations of thinkers of many years past, and still possesses sufficient vitality to affect those whose minds are ready to receive them at this time. And we all attract to us thought vibrations corresponding in nature with those which we are in the habit of entertaining. The Law of Attraction is in full operation, and one who makes a study of the subject may see instances of it on all sides.

We invite to ourselves these thought vibrations by maintaining and entertaining thoughts along certain lines. If we cultivate a habit of thinking along the lines of Cheerfulness, Brightness and Optimism, we attract to ourselves similar thought vibrations of others and we will find that before long we will find all sorts of cheerful thoughts pouring into our minds from all directions. And, likewise, if we harbor thoughts of Gloom, Despair, Pessimism, we lay ourselves open to the influx of similar thoughts which have emanated from the minds of others. Thoughts of Anger, Hate, or Jealousy attract similar thoughts which serve to feed the flame and keep alive the fire of these low emotions. Thoughts of Love tend to draw to ourselves the loving thoughts of others which tend to fill us with a glow of loving emotion.

And not only are we affected in this way by the thoughts of others, but what is known as "Suggestion" also plays an important part in this matter of subconscious influence. We find that the mind has a tendency to reproduce the emotions, moods, shades of thought, and feelings of other persons, as evidenced by their attitude, appearance, facial expression, or words. If we associate with persons of a gloomy temperament, we run the risk of "catching" their mental trouble by the law of suggestion, unless we understand this law and counter-act it. In the same way we find that cheerfulness is conta-gious, and if we keep in the company of cheerful people we are very apt to take on their mental quality. The same rule ap-plies to frequenting the company of unsuccessful or success-ful people, as the case may be. If we allow ourselves to take up the suggestions constantly emanating from them, we will find that our minds will begin to reproduce the tones, atti-tudes, characteristics, dispositions and traits of the other per-sons, and before long we will be living on the same mental plane. As we have repeatedly said, these things are true only when we allow ourselves to "take on" the impressions, but un-less one has mastered the law of suggestion, and understands its principles and operations he is more or less apt to be affect-ed by it. All of you readily recall the effect of certain persons upon others with whom they come in contact. One has a fac-ulty of inspiring with vigor and energy those in whose com-pany he happens to be. Another depresses those around him, and is avoided as a "human wet blanket." Another will cause a feeling of uneasiness in those around him, by reason of his prevailing attitude of distrust, suspicion, and low cunning.

Some carry an atmosphere of health around them, while others seem to be surrounded with a sickly aura of disease, even when their physical condition does not seem to indicate the lack of health. Mental states have a subtle way of impressing themselves upon us, and the student who will take the trouble to closely observe those with whom he comes in contact will receive a liberal education along these lines.

There is of course a great difference in the degree of suggestibility among different persons. There are those who are almost immune, while at the other end of the line are to be found others who are so constantly and strongly impressed by the suggestions of others, conscious or unconscious, that they may be said to scarcely have any independent thought or will of their own. But nearly all persons are suggestible to a greater or lesser degree.

It must not be supposed from what we have said that all suggestions are "bad," harmful, or undesirable. Many suggestions are very good for us, and coming at the right time have aided us much. But, nevertheless, it is well to always *let your own mind pass upon* these suggestions, before allowing them to manifest in your subconscious mind. Let the final decision be your own—and not the will of another—although you may have considered outside suggestions in connection with the matter.

Remember always that YOU are an Individual, having a mind and Will of your own. Rest firmly upon the base of your "I" consciousness, and you will find yourself able to manifest a wonderful strength against the adverse suggestions of others. Be your own Suggestor—train and influence your subconscious mind Yourself, and do not allow it to be tampered with by the suggestions of others. Grow the sense of Individuality.

There has been much written of recent years in the Western world regarding the effect of the Mental Attitude upon Success and attainment upon the material plane. While much of this is nothing but the wildest imagining, still there remains a very firm and solid substratum of truth underlying it all.

It is undoubtedly true that one's prevailing mental attitude is constantly manifesting and objectifying itself in his life. Things, circumstances, people, plans, all seem to fit into the general ideal of the strong mental attitude of a man. And this from the operation of mental law along a number of lines of action.

In the first place, the mind when directed toward a certain set of objects becomes very alert to discover things concerning those objects—to seize upon things, opportunities, persons, ideas, and facts tending to promote the objects thought of. The man who is looking for facts to prove certain theories, invariably finds them, and is also quite likely to overlook facts tending to disprove his theory. The Optimist and the Pessimist passing along the same streets, each sees thousands of examples tending to fit in with his idea. As Kay says: "When one is engaged in seeking for a thing, if he keep the image of it clearly before the mind, he will be very likely to find it, and that too, probably, where it would otherwise have escaped his notice. So when one is engaged in thinking on a subject, thoughts of things resembling it, or bearing upon it, and tending to illustrate it, come up on every side. Truly, we may well say of the mind, as has been said of the eye, that 'it perceives only what it brings within the power of perceiving.'" John Burroughs has well said regarding this that "No one ever found the walking fern who did not have the walking fern in his mind. A person whose eye is full of

Indian relics picks them up in every field he walks through. They are quickly recognized because the eye has been commissioned to find them."

When the mind is kept firmly fixed upon some ideal or aim, its whole and varied powers are bent toward the realization and manifestation of that ideal. In thousands of ways the mind will operate to objectify the subjective mental attitude, a great proportion of the mental effort being accomplished along subconscious lines. It is of the greatest importance to one who wishes to succeed in any undertaking, to keep before his mind's eye a clear mental image of that which he desires. He should picture the thing desired, and himself as securing it, until it becomes almost real. In this way he calls to his aid his entire mental force and power, along the subconscious lines, and, as it were, makes a clear path over which he may walk to accomplishment. Bain says regarding this: "By aiming at a new construction, we must clearly conceive what is aimed at. Where we have a very distinct and intelligible model before us, we are in a fair way to succeed; in proportion as the ideal is dim and wavering, we stagger or miscarry." Maudsley says: "We cannot do an act voluntarily unless we know what we are going to do, and we cannot know exactly what we are going to do until we have taught ourselves to do it." Carpenter says: "The continued concentration of attention upon a certain idea gives it a dominant power, not only over the mind, but over the body." Müller says: "The idea of our own strength gives strength to our movements. A person who is confident of effecting anything by muscular efforts will do it more easily than one not so confident of his own power." Tanner says: "To believe firmly is almost tantamount in the end to accomplishment. Extraordinary instances are related showing the influence of the will over even the involuntary muscles."

Along the same lines, many Western writers have added their testimony to the Yogi principle of the manifestation of thought into action. Kay has written: "A clear and accurate idea of what we wish to do, and how it is to be effected, is of the utmost value and importance in all the affairs of life. A man's conduct naturally shapes itself according to the ideas in his mind, and nothing contributes more to success in life than having a high ideal and keeping it constantly in view. Where such is the case one can hardly fail in attaining it. Numerous unexpected circumstances will be found to conspire to bring it about, and even what seemed at first to be hostile may be converted into means for its furtherance; while by having it constantly before the mind he will be ever ready to take advantage of any favoring circumstances that may present themselves." Along the same lines, Foster has written these remarkable words: "It is wonderful how even the casualties of life seem to bow to a spirit that will not bow to them, and yield to subserve a design which they may, in their first apparent tendency, threaten to frustrate. When a firm, decisive spirit is recognized, it is curious to see how the space clears around a man and leaves him room and freedom." Simpson has said: "A passionate desire and an unwearied will can perform impossibilities, or what seem to be such to the cold and feeble." And Maudsley gives to aspiring youth a great truth, when he says: "Thus it is that aspirations are often prophecies, the harbingers of what a man shall be in a condition to perform." And we may conclude the paragraph by quoting Lytton: "Dream, O youth, dream manfully and nobly, and thy dreams shall be prophets."

This principle of the power of the Mental Image is strongly impressed upon the mind of the *chela*, or student, by the Yogi teachers. The student is taught that just as the house is erected in accordance with the plan of the architect, so is one's life built in accordance with the prevailing Mental Image. The mind subconsciously moulds itself around the prevailing mental image or attitude, and then proceeds to draw upon the outer world for material with which to build in accordance with the plan. Not only is one's character built in this way, but the circumstances and incidents of his life follow the same rule. The Yogi student is instructed into the mysteries of the power of the mind in this direction, not that he may make use of it to build up material success, or to realize his personal desires—for he is taught to avoid these things—but he is fully instructed, nevertheless, that he may understand the workings of the law around him. And it is a fact well known to close students of the occult, that the few who have attained extraordinarily high degrees of development, make use of this power in order to help the race. Many a world movement has been directed by the mind, or minds, of some of these advanced souls who were able to see the ideal of evolution ahead of the race, and by visualizing the same, and concentrating upon it in meditation, actually hastened the progress of the evolutionary wave, and caused to actually manifest that which they saw, and upon which they had meditated.

It is true that some occultists have used similar plans to further their own selfish personal ends—often without fully realizing just what power they were employing—but this merely illustrates the old fact that the forces of Nature may be used rightly and wrongly. And it is all the more reason why those who are desirous of advancing the race—of assisting in the evolution of the world—should make use of this mighty power in their work. Success is not reprehensible, notwithstanding the fact that many have interpreted and applied the word in such a matter as to make it appear as if it had no other meaning or application other than the crude, material selfish one generally attributed to it, by reason of its misuse. The Western world is playing its part in the evolution of the race, and its keynote is "Accomplishment." Those who have advanced so high that they are able to view the world of men, as one sees a valley from a mountain peak, recognize what this strenuous Western life means. They see mighty forces in operation—mighty principles being worked out by those who little dream of the ultimate significance of that which they are doing. Mighty things are before the Western world today—wonderful changes are going on—great things are in the womb of time, and the hour of birth draws near. The men and women in the Western world feel within them the mighty urge to "accomplish" something—to take an active part in the great drama of life. And they are right in giving full expression to this urge, and are doing well in using every legitimate means in the line of expression. And this idea of the Mental Attitude, or the Mental Image, is one of the greatest factors in this striving for Success.

In this lesson we do not purpose giving "Success Talks" for our students. These lessons are intended to fill another field, and there are many other channels of information along the lines named. What we wish to do is to point out to our students the meaning of all this strenuous striving of the age, in the Western world, and the leading principle employed therein. The great achievements of the material world are being accomplished by means of the Power of the Mind. Men are beginning to understand that "Thought manifests itself in Action," and that Thought attracts to itself the things, persons and circumstances in harmony with itself. The Power of Mind is becoming manifest in hundreds of ways. The power of Desire, backed by Faith and Will, is beginning to be recognized as one of the greatest of known dynamic forces. The life of the race is entering into a new and strange stage of development and evolution, and in the years to come MIND will be seen, more clearly and still more clearly, to be the great principle underlying the world of material things and happenings. That "All is Mind" is more than a dreamy, metaphysical utterance, is being recognized by the leaders in the world's thought.

As we have said, great changes are before the world and the race, and every year brings us nearer to the beginning of them. In fact, the beginning is already upon us. Let any thinker stop and reflect over the wonderful changes of the past six years—since the dawning of the Twentieth Century, and he will be dull indeed if he sees not the trend of affairs. We are entering into a new Great Cycle of the race, and the old is being prepared for being dropped off like an old worn-out husk. Old conventions, ideals, customs, laws, ethics, and things sociological, economical, theological, philosophical, and metaphysical have been outgrown, and are about to be "shed" by the race. The great cauldron of human thought is bubbling away fiercely, and many things are rising to its surface. Like all great changes, the good will come only with much pain—all birth is with pain. The race feels the pain and perpetual unrest, but knows not what is the disease nor the remedy. Many false cases of diagnosis and prescription are even now noticeable, and will become still more in evidence as the years roll by. Many self-styled saviours of the race—prescribers for the pain of the soul and mind—will arise and fall. But out of it all will come that for which the race now waits.

The changes that are before us are as great as the changes in thought and life described in the late novel by H. G. Wells,[10] entitled *In the Days of the Comet*. In fact, Mr. Wells has indicated in that story some of the very changes that the advanced souls of the race have informed their students are before the race—the prophetic insight of the writer named seems marvelous, until one realizes that even that writer is being used as a part of the mental machinery of The Change itself. But the change will not come about by reason of the new gas caused by the brushing of the earth's surface by a passing comet. It will come from the unfolding of the race mind, the process being now underway. Are not the signs of mental unrest and discomfort becoming more and more apparent as the days go by? The pain is growing greater, and the race is beginning to fret and chafe, and moan. It knows not what it wants, but it knows that it feels pain and wants something to relieve that pain. The old things are beginning to totter and fall, and ideas rendered sacred by years of observance are being brushed aside with a startling display of irreverence. Under the surface of our civilization we may hear the straining and groaning of the ideas and principles that are striving to force their way out on to the plane of manifestation.

Men are running hither and thither crying for a leader and a savior. They are trying this thing, and that thing, but they find not that which they seek. They cry for Satisfaction, but it eludes them. And yet all this search and disappointment is part of the Great Change, and is preparing the race for That-which-must-Come. And yet the relief will not come from any Thing or Things. It will come from Within. Just as when, in Well's story, things righted themselves when the vapor of the comet had cleared men's minds, so will Things take their new places when the mind of the race becomes cleared by the new unfoldment that is even now under way. Men are beginning to feel each other's pains—they find themselves unsatisfied by the old rule of "every man for himself, and the devil take the hindmost"—it used to content the successful, but now it doesn't seem to be so satisfying. The man on top is becoming lonesome, and dissatisfied, and discontented—his success seems to appall him, in some mysterious manner. And the man underneath feels stirring within himself strange longings and desires, and dissatisfaction. And new frictions are arising, and new and startling ideas are being suddenly advanced, supported and opposed.

And the relations between people seem to be unsatisfactory. The old rules, laws, and bonds are proving irksome. New, strange, and wild thoughts are coming into the minds of people, which they dare not utter to their friends—and yet these same friends are finding similar ideas within themselves. And somehow, underneath it all is to be found a certain Honesty—yes, there is where the trouble seems to come, *the world is tiring of hypocrisy and dishonesty in all human relations,* and is crying aloud to be led back, someway, to Truth and Honesty in Thought and Action. But it does not see the way out! And it will not see the way out, until the race-mind unfolds still further. And the pain of the new unfoldment is stirring the race to its depths. From the deep recesses of the race-mind are rising to the surface old passions, relics from the cave-dweller days, and all sorts of ugly mental relics of the past. And they will continue to rise and show themselves until at last the bubbling pot will begin to quiet down, and then will come a new peace, and the best will come to the surface—the essence of all the experiences of the race.

To our students, we would say: During the struggle ahead of the race, play well your part, doing the best you can, living each day by itself, meeting each new phase of life with confidence and courage. Be not deluded by appearances, nor follow after strange prophets. Let the evolutionary processes work themselves out, and do you fall in with the wave without struggling, and without overmuch striving. The Law is working itself out well—of that be assured. Those who have entered into even a partial understanding and recognition of the One Life underlying, will find that they will be as the chosen people during the changes that are coming to the race. They have attained that which the race is reaching toward in pain and travail. And the force behind the Law will carry them along, for they will be the leaven that is to lighten the great mass of the race in the new dispensation. Not by deed, or by action, but by Thought, will these people leaven the mass. The Thought is even now at work, and all who read these words are playing a part in the work, although they may know it not. If the race could realize this truth of the One Life underlying, today, the Change would occur in a moment, but it will not come in that way. When this understanding gradually dawns upon the race—this new consciousness—then will Things take their proper places, and the Lion and the Lamb lie down together in peace.

We have thought it well to say these things in this the last lesson of this course. They are needed words—they will serve to point out the way to those who are able to read. *"Watch and wait for the Silence that will follow the Storm."*

In this series of lessons we have endeavored to give you a plain, practical presentation of some of the more important features of Raja Yoga. But this phase of the subject, as important and interesting as it is, is not the highest phase of the great Yoga teachings. It is merely the preparation of the soil of the mind for what comes afterward. The phase called "Gnani Yoga"—the Yoga of Wisdom—is the highest of all the various phases of Yoga, although each of the lower steps is important in itself. We find ourselves approaching the phase of our work for which we have long wished. Those who have advised and directed this work have counseled us to deal with the less advanced and simpler phases, in order to prepare the minds of those who might be interested, so that they would be ready for the higher teachings. At times we have felt an impatience for the coming of the day when we would be able to teach the highest that has come to us. And now the time seems to have come. Following this course, we will begin a series of lessons in "GNANI YOGA"—the Yoga of Wisdom—in which we will pass on to our students the highest teachings regarding the Reality and its Manifestations—the One and the Many. The teachings that "All is Mind" will be explained in such a manner as to be understood by all who have followed us so far. We will be able to impart to you the higher truths about Spiritual Evolution, sometimes called "Reincarnation," as well as Spiritual Cause and Effect, often called "Karma." The highest truths about these important subjects are often obscured by popular misconceptions occasioned by partial teaching. We trust that you—our students—will wish to follow us still higher—higher than we have ventured so far, and we assure you that there is a Truth to be seen and known that is as much higher than the other phases upon which we have touched, as those phases have been higher than the current beliefs of the masses of the race. We trust that the Powers of Knowledge may guide and direct us that we may be able to convey our message so that it may be accepted and understood. We thank our students who have traveled thus far with us, and we assure them that their loving sympathy has ever been a help and an inspiration to us.

Peace be with you.

Endnotes

FIRST LESSON

1   In the early part of the twentieth century, the world was still en-
     meshed in colonialism. The prevailing attitude minimized in-
     digenous world cultures, often referring to nonwhite people pe-
     joratively as "savages" or "barbarians." Indigenous cultures were
     misunderstood, largely unknown, and thought to be "uncivilized"
     or "primitive" due to their not having partaken of the technological
     and scientific achievements of more advanced societies. It is within
     this context—decades before the proliferation of cultural sensitiv-
     ity—that the present author or authors used such adjectives when
     alluding to indigenous cultures.

SECOND LESSON

2   Edward Carpenter (1844-1929) was an English socialist, poet, phi-
     losopher, and early activist for gay and animal rights. He traveled
     to India and Sri Lanka in 1890 to study Hindu philosophy. These
     travels inspired his book *From Adam's Peak to Elephanta: Sketches
     of Ceylon and India*, originally published in 1892.

THIRD LESSON

3   Mabel Collins (1851-1927), also known as "M.C.," was a theoso-
     phist writer who penned several articles and forty-six books, the
     most influential of which was the short book *Light on the Path* pub-
     lished in 1885.

4 Hermann Ludwig Ferdinand von Helmholtz (1821-1894) was one of the greatest German physicists and physicians of the nineteenth century. His research led to many discoveries on a wide range of subjects, including electromagnetism, mechanics, optics, sensory physiology, ophthalmology, and nerve physiology.

5 Herbert Spencer (1820-1903) was an English philosopher, biologist, sociologist, political theorist, and one of the founders of Social Darwinism. He is the person who coined the phrase "survival of the fittest."

SEVENTH LESSON

6 Ernst Haeckel (1834-1919) was a German zoologist, naturalist, philosopher, and one of the most influential scientists of the nineteenth century. He discovered thousands of new species, created many genealogical trees relating all life-forms, and named and classified many animals. He introduced important new terms in biology, including "phylum," "Protista," and "ecology." Haeckel proposed the famous recapitulation theory ("ontogeny recapitulates phylogeny"), which claims that an individual organism's biological development, or ontogeny, parallels its species' evolutionary development, or phylogeny. In 1904, he published *The Wonders of Life: A Popular Study of Biological Philosophy*, which explores the theory of evolution and the origins of life. He also promoted and popularized Darwin's theory in Germany.

7 Richard Maurice Burke (1837-1902) was a Canadian psychiatrist and writer who wrote *Cosmic Consciousness: A Study in the Evolution of the Human Mind*, published in 1901. This researched compilation of different theories describes the mystical experiences of historical figures such as the Buddha and Jesus, as well as some of his contemporaries such as Walt Whitman. He borrowed the term

"cosmic consciousness" from his friend Edward Carpenter, who had traveled to India to study religion.

8 Walter "Walt" Whitman (1819-1892) is one of the most influential American poets. His groundbreaking book *Leaves of Grass*, a collection of poems, was originally published in 1855.

EIGHTH LESSON

9 Oliver Wendell Holmes, Sr. (1809-1894) was a Bostonian physician, poet, and polymath. He was considered one of the best writers of his time; among his work is the *Breakfast-Table* series, a collection of philosophically oriented essays that address diverse themes such as the benefits of old age and the perfect site to build a home. These essays were originally published in the *Atlantic Monthly* magazine and subsequently in book form.

TWELFTH LESSON

10 Herbert George "H.G." Wells (1866-1946) was an English writer and futurist who is best known for his science fiction novels, most notably *The War of the Worlds*. His book *In the Days of the Comet* (1906) is about a comet that changes the atmosphere and creates a more peaceful and beautiful society.

THE BOOK *A SERIES OF LESSONS IN RAJA YOGA* BY YOGI RAMACHARAKA WAS EDITED BY JANE KAYANTAS, PROOFREAD BY THE RED TO BLACK EDITING COMPANY, DESIGNED BY POPPY ALEXIOU, PRINTED AND BOUND BY BANG PRINTING ON TRADEBOOK NATURAL #50 PAPER IN 3000 COPIES ON BEHALF OF BAMBOO LEAF PRESS

NOW AVAILABLE

The first book of the Yogi Ramacharaka series.

FOURTEEN LESSONS IN YOGI PHILOSOPHY

YOGI RAMACHARAKA

WITH A NEW FOREWORD BY RICHARD ROSEN

ISBN 978-0-9974148-3-7
eBook ISBN 978-0-9974148-4-4

NOW AVAILABLE

The second book of the Yogi Ramacharaka series.

ADVANCED COURSE IN YOGI PHILOSOPHY

YOGI RAMACHARAKA

WITH A NEW FOREWORD BY RICHARD ROSEN

ISBN 978-0-9974148-5-1
eBook ISBN 978-0-9974148-6-8